S0-BED-253

Pantheon Books ☐ 1979

Kids' Stuff

Linda Foa & Geri Brin
Photography by Michael Datoli

GRAPHIC CREDITS:

ART DIRECTOR & DESIGNER:
Janet Odgis

GRAPHIC DIRECTOR:
Bob Scudellari

PRODUCTION DIRECTOR:
Constance Mellon

TYPESETTING & COMPOSITION:
Superior Printing

TEXT PRINTING:
The Murray Printing Company

COLOR SEPARATIONS:
Beaumont Graphics

COLOR PRINTING:
Einson Freeman Graphics

BINDING:
The Murray Printing Company

This book is dedicated to
Husbands Conrad Foa and Douglas Brin
The Foa boys—Justin and Barrett
And a soon-to-be-born Brin who will
undoubtedly benefit from *KIDS' STUFF*

Library of Congress Cataloging in Publication Data

Foa, Linda, 1942-
Kids' Stuff.

1. Children's furniture—Catalogs. 2. Children's
paraphernalia—Catalogs. I. Brin, Geri, 1947-
joint author. II. Title.
TT197.5.C5F63   684   78-14343
ISBN 0-394-41558-2   ISBN 0-394-73658-3 pbk.

Manufactured in the United States of America

FIRST EDITION

KIDS' STUFF

Acknowledgments

Two years of work went into this book, involving the cooperation of hundreds of people: manufacturers who believed enough in our project to ship their merchandise for photography; designers, educators, psychologists, retailers, and everyone else who devoted their valuable time for interviews; family and friends who patiently listened to and supported us. We are grateful to all those who haven't forgotten what it's like to be a kid.

We obviously cannot thank everyone by name, but we would like to single out a group of very special people. We are grateful to Pat Ross, the Knopf editor who introduced us to Pantheon; designer Joe D'Urso, whose invaluable advice and knowledge helped define the book; Arlene Hirst, for her enthusiasm and merchandising know-how; Stephen A. Miller, toy maven, who led us to many exciting resources; Charles Bunting, from Novo Toys; architects Bob Mayers and John Schiff; Maynard Lyndon, owner of Massachusetts's Plum Loco; Jerry Samet, who ably assisted photographer Michael Datoli; Klaus Moser Lab; and Kathy Perucci and her spacious van.

Thanks also to those retailers who quickly got merchandise to us: The Workbench, Hammacher Schlemmer, Design Research, Bailey Hubner at Henri Bendel, Novo Toys, Albee and Ben's, Schacters, and Schneider's.

And our biggest thanks to our editor at Pantheon, Barbara Plumb, whose excitement and insights were rewarding; to Janet Odgis, the award-winning Pantheon designer who gave her love and talent to *Kids' Stuff*; and to Phyllis Benjamin, who edited the text and checked every detail patiently and professionally.

Last, but certainly not least, our love and gratitude to those dearest to us who lived through this *Kids' Stuff* experience: Douglas Brin; Conrad, Justin and Barrett Foa; David Bradescu; and Ray Wilson. And to our parents, who made us kids in the first place: May and Samuel Goldberg, Grace and Sam Rimanich, and Mary and Albert Datoli.

Preface

If you're looking for the most convenient carriage for your new baby . . . the sturdiest desk for your seven- or seventeen-year-old . . . the best bunk bed for your ten-year-old . . . the most practical swing set . . . and lots of versatile storage units for all your kids' possessions, no matter how old they are . . . *Kids' Stuff* is just right for you.

This book is not going to tell you how to deal with teething, toilet training, and tempers. It's not even going to teach you how to decorate your child's room or how to build furniture. But it will offer you three hundred specific items in eight key home-furnishings categories important to the smooth interaction between children and their environment. It talks about how children like to sit, sleep, eat, work, and play—everything they normally do—and it tells how certain pieces of equipment can help them do it better.

This is a catalog of stuff for little kids and big kids: bunk beds and sleeping bags, cribs and carriages, cots and jungle gyms, worktables and adjustable stools. Furnishing your children with the right equipment can be just as important as furnishing them with the proper care, because the right equipment saves time, money, space, and aggravation, making life easier for everyone.

Every piece of merchandise has been chosen in terms of function, versatility, good design, and durability. Much of it works as well for adults as for children. We like to think of these three hundred items as the cream of the crop. Many of them have been recommended by designers, psychologists, educators, and parents—people who work closely with kids and know what they like and what they need.

The catalog is easy to use. Each item is accompanied by a caption explaining what it's made of, its sizes, and how it will fit into your child's life and yours. Following the description is the manufacturer's address and the item's suggested retail price. When you find something you like, write to the manufacturer and he'll be glad to tell you where to purchase the item in your area. In some cases, you may want to request a manufacturer's entire catalog.

Much of the merchandise in this book can be purchased for less than the suggested retail price listed. The price you pay may vary depending on your agreement with a dealer, designer, decorator, or architect. Once you've written to the manufacturer—and he's told you where to go—you can work on getting the best prices.

Prices have been estimated for the time of publication of this book, although costs of materials and labor may cause them to rise six months from now. We do, however, want you to know whether something is five, fifty, or two hundred dollars.

Some of the equipment will be familiar and easy to find—things like Cosco's booster seat, Simmons's crib, Rubbermaid's wastebaskets, and Norelco's ice cream maker. But lots of items will be totally new to you, from companies you've probably never heard of—things like Shure's rolling tool chest, United Metal's storage dome, Sico's folding worktable, or Akro-Mils' colorful storage bins.

You've probably never heard of many of these companies because they do not deal directly with conventional retail outlets but rather with the industrial, institutional, school, or contract markets. Republic Steel, for instance, sells its shelves to libraries, but they'll work just as beautifully at home. Hotels use Harloff's metal totes to transport cleaning supplies, but your kids will love them for all their toys. And Tucker Duck and Rubber sells its cots to schools, but there's no reason why your youngster can't have one in his or her playroom.

We've gone to all these unusual sources simply because there's a dearth of good, well-made, conventional children's merchandise. One big retailer even told us: "There's so little around that's worth selling in my kids' department." Too often conventional kids' stuff is more concerned with decals than with function and durability.

Generally, the things you can count on with industrial, school, or contract merchandise are durability and clean design. A table or chair designed for schools will normally stand up to a lot more abuse than one designed for the home. A heavy-duty rubber mat made for offices will certainly be able to handle a group of kids messing around on the floor.

Bear in mind, however, that price and quality often go hand in hand. A well-made steel shelving unit may cost more than a flimsy one but will be well worth the investment if you're interested in having it last a long time. Children need sturdy merchandise.

Besides, think of how much you spend on toys during your child's first ten years. Many of them cost $25 and fall apart within a few weeks. Why not invest a few dollars more and buy your child a tent, sleeping bag, or great indoor jungle gym? We can almost assure you they'll love it as much as a toy... and for a lot longer, too.

We hope this book will inspire you to look at new ways to equip your child's environment. What we've done is provided you with the sources. It's up to you to do the rest.

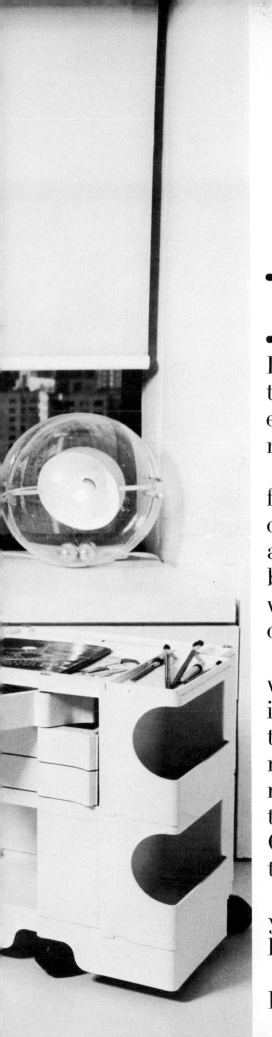

Environments

Before you start looking and reading through these pages for new ways to equip your child's environment, think about the big picture: a naked room.

Almost every space, no matter how small, has four fixed architectural elements: walls, floor, ceiling, and windows. Just because these elements are automatically there doesn't mean they should be ignored. Children relate to walls, floors and windows long before they need a small rocking chair, walker, or place to store their possessions.

The covering that goes on a floor, the paint on a wall, or the shade on a window can be a big factor in a child's early stimulation. The treatment of these elements most often sets the tone of the environment. The child, and later the adult, should be master of his surroundings. Space should be neutral enough for a child to move easily through it. Children—not the walls or floor—should provide the color.

Children adore the floor. How many times have you seen a room filled with chairs, and all the little bottoms seated on the floor?

The floor is congenial to the child's development. It is his substitute for tables and chairs—his furniture — and it should be as appealing as grass. It's a child's first exposure to the world outside the crib.

Youngsters from one to two and a half don't need chairs. Chair sitting is a social thing that little kids don't love. Any child fits the floor and the floor fits any child. "It is a critical element and should be considered right off, as soon as the youngster starts traveling on all fours," says Nancy Rambusch, director of New York City's Caedmon School.

There are fewer than a handful of things to consider when deciding what flooring is good for a child's bed or playroom: it must be free from drafts and warm to the touch so the child will be comfortable when playing; it should be easy to maintain; minimize slipping hazards, and prevent germ retention; it should be resilient to minimize accidents from falls, muffle sound, and be adaptable for both work and play.

Resilient flooring and carpeting each satisfy some of these criteria, but neither satisfies all. Vinyl tile is easy to clean, but not exactly warm to the touch. "It's like grass covered with snow," Ms. Rambusch says. Carpeting is soft and comfortable, has great sound-absorbing qualities, and reduces accidents from falls, but is harder to keep clean.

There are advocates on both sides. Designer Noel Jeffrey really doesn't approve of carpeting in a kid's room and prefers a polyurethaned wood floor because it's wipeable. Alexandra Stoddard, in her book *A Child's Place*, says wall-to-wall carpeting, with few exceptions, is expensive, limiting, and a problem to keep clean. She prefers area rugs over a wood or vinyl floor. But Nancy Rambusch says: "Never leave carpet out totally." She prefers

low-pile carpet to something like shag because it's easier to clean and also muffles sound.

One of the most practical and often ignored possibilities is to carpet part of the room and do the remaining surface in vinyl. That way kids can use one part for wet, rugged, or messy activities like painting, and the carpeted part for more "tidy" activities like reading, writing, or tumbling. You might even provide little squares of portable carpet for the vinyl-covered floor, since kids often like to set their work on them. "The carpet square defines a space more easily than the whole floor," notes Robin Berenstain, who runs a Denver daycare center. A little child can sit on one end of a 2-foot by 2-foot carpet sample and put his Legos on the other end.

If you'd prefer to carpet the whole floor, another way to cater to messy activities is by putting down big mats of smooth vinyl or rubber similar to those often found under office chairs. These can be moved wherever you want so your child can paint in any room without your having to keep telling him to "keep clean."

Many designers and educators like neutral-color carpet best because everything reads well against it. Work done on the floor should be easily seen by the child.

The floor opens up other creative possibilities:
•Extend the floor by carpeting raised areas. Nancy Rambusch did this in one school with movable rectangular prisms. "These established limits without trapping the children and did what the playpen does poorly. They're barriers that aren't perceived as barriers," she explains. Children would take a number of prisms and create their own work/play platforms. The prisms are a big

improvement over tables and chairs because they permit the child to perform in many postures. If there are many acceptable surfaces on which to work, squat, kneel, stand, or lie down, then the child can focus on the business at hand. •Carpet "steps leading to nowhere," as did the Acorn School in New York. Kids love to climb to the top step to sit and read. •Make tiny 9-inch-square pillows—lots of them covered in varying textures. Kids will pile them in a corner and plop down over them. They love to use their bodies on the floor. Pillows and platforms let children do a lot with very little. Furniture is kept to a minimum. "Small children often have too much furniture," notes Larry Malloy of Educational Facilities Labs. "Space for small people is often better unfilled." •Create "sunken" areas in the floor for kids to play in. • Stain the part of the floor left uncovered by carpet —if it's wood. Light-color stains look clean and fresh. Dark colors, like red, may be attractive, but they will easily show scuffs, chips, and scratches.

The ceiling is one of the biggest unused portions of space in the house. Unfortunately. Yes, it's true kids don't crawl or work on the ceiling, or even relate to it until they develop a three dimensional sense. But once they do, there's no reason why the ceiling can't be utilized.

One young boy started dealing with vertical space when he climbed to the top of his bunk bed. The ceiling was his new discovery, and since he collects maps, he decided to put one on the ceiling right over the bed. Now he lies in bed and studies the map before going to sleep. Another five-year-old hung his 6-foot Superman figure on the ceiling so it looks as if Superman's flying. He loves it.

1. People who own Palaset become committed to its fantastic flexibility. Cubes and drawers, used individually or in multiples, can be clipped and stacked together to form work or play environments all over the house. Each element is made of structural polystyrene plastic—you can nail, saw, drill, and paint it just like wood.

There are many ways to use Palaset. You might want to design a desk, a bathroom vanity, a platform bed. Adults, no doubt, will have fun putting it together. Basic cabinets are 13 inches per side in white or brown; drawers are available in red, yellow, or green.

We've created a play center that focuses on a child's favorite place: the floor. He can happily roll around on the Everlast gym mats, straddle the Everlast punching bag, and grab every-thing he needs from the open Palaset units. The structure should be kept low for young children so they won't have to reach too far. But later on, Palaset can grow with them. Here the three-sided enclosure also provides a sense of security.

A hanging fixture by Abolite sheds light on the environment.

Conran's: The Market at Citicorp Center, 160 East 54 Street, New York, New York 10022; or
Dania Imports: 407 North Anaheim Boulevard, Orange, California 92668 $22.50—open cube; $24.50—cube with one shelf; $33.00—cube with door; $35.00—cube with door and shelf; $9.00—drawer; $7.00—narrow drawer (dealer)
Treston Oy.: Sorakatu 1; SF-207200; Turku 72 Finland (mfg.)

2. A child's bedroom should be more than just a place to sleep, according to designer John Saladino. It should expand the possibilities of other worlds... stimulate the imagination. "It's always easier," Saladino says, "to be more imaginative when creating a child's room." And he has developed an environment (here) that Alice in Wonderland would have loved.

It has a gray Formica ramp, overscaled shelves, cubbies, and a raised Formica platform so the child can see the glorious view when she's seated at the desk. The platform and ramp can be removed when she grows up.

There are places to slide, hide, tumble, and climb. And—like Alice—the little girl can have a friend over for a tea party at the plastic laminate white desk. It features a semicircle extension for the cups, saucers, and teapot. The girls can sit on India Nepal's rattan stools.

A "staircase" to the left of the bed leads to nowhere; it makes a good climbing mountain. These large step-up cubes hold lots and lots of toys or little children, so they can also become pirates' hideouts. Later on, they'll work for book or clothes storage. More storage space is provided in the three drawers under the bed.

Although Saladino usually prefers a hard surface floor ("for spills") covered with removable carpeting ("for easy cleaning"), he decided to do this room entirely in gray Pirelli rubber tiles. Even the storage bins are topped with Pirelli. The washable flooring responds well to scooters, doll buggies, and all-around kids' stuff. Besides, the well-known raised geometrics look beautiful. (continued on page 21)

The walls are mostly cork painted in white or highway-stripe yellow. "They're great for hanging posters, artwork, or notes," Saladino says. Clamp lights are positioned on one of the oversized shelves above the bed, ready for when the child wants a bedtime story. A Teddy Roosevelt-style hunting chair is covered with soft pink, just like the bed and stools. It's all rather fanciful . . . and functional as well.

John F. Saladino Inc.: 305 East 63 Street, Penthouse, New York, New York 10021

3. Judy Colton decided to put Muurame furniture in her son's rather compact room because she likes its practicality. "The drawers and shelves are deep and the look is classic and clean," she says.

The spacious white birch unit combines open and closed storage. Clothes go in the six-drawer chest; books, records, firehats, and footballs go on the four shelves; and anything left over hides behind the two cabinets below.

The rest of the sensibly planned room features more storage and loads of bright, primary color.

Akro-Mils's roomy bins in red, blue, and yellow sit on top of the desk, along with a black Luxo lamp and a Palaset storage cube with three red drawers. Bigger bins hold toys in the chest below. Cramer's red Kik Step Stool is ready to help a child reach a top shelf.

One side of the Muurame desk is supported by a base and the other by a hidden piece of plywood between the chest and the top. "It almost looks like it's floating," Judy says. Castelli's Box Chair, in bright yellow, waits for homework time.

4. Over 53,000 yards of Decathlon carpeting cover the New Orleans Superdome, where millions walk and run over it every year. Think how well it should stand up in a kid's playroom, preceding page, or bedroom (which sometimes seems like a sports arena itself). Decathlon is a low-pile industrial grade carpet made of one hundred percent Vectra fiber. It's designed to withstand the toughest activity and backed by a five-year wear guarantee.

It is available with either a jute or a foam back; we recommend the jute for children's rooms, since it performs better and is generally stronger. Comes in beautiful muted heather colors, including brown tea, brown lacquer, emperor blue, rustic, and coal. The carpet's nonstatic qualities make it especially comfortable.

Wellco Carpet Corp.: P.O. Box 281, Calhoun, Georgia 30701 $10 per yard—with jute backing; $11—with foam backing

Designer Noel Jeffrey painted a blue circle with white clouds right in the center of the ceiling in one child's room so it looks like a skylight. "People are always forgetting that space," Mr. Jeffrey says. A rubber balloon can be suspended from the ceiling and used as a punching bag to release a child's frustrations. The Rusk Institute in New York City does this to develop muscular skills in handicapped children, but it will work well for any child. "Anything hanging from the ceiling is exciting," thinks designer Ward Bennett.

On the other hand, a child starts relating to the walls right away, and they can be a source of visual stimulation to the baby in her crib. Walls also lend a sense of security to an infant. Later, when the walls become a barricade to the toddler, she will want to touch them and write on them.

Walls are best painted white or in tones of white. High-gloss paint is best because it gives a rich-looking lacquered quality to ceiling and walls and is easy to wipe down. "Kids like color very much and parents therefore think the room should be bright red, blue, or yellow. Colored walls drive kids nuts. They're not restful," says Robin Berenstain, who instead prefers neutral walls. It is all the objects of childhood—the toys and books, the working and playing materials—that provide the color kids love. Nothing looks more cheerful than colored storage bins filled with crayons and toys and set against a white wall.

There are other ways to add excitement to the walls without painting them red or hanging up Little Bo Peep wallpaper. Put cutout letters of the alphabet across one wall; or ten circles so your child will learn how to count; or ten butterflies. A kite hung on the wall with a child's name on it could also be appealing. Children might even grow up with an appreciation for good art if it hangs on their walls from the time they're little. Every museum sells inexpensive prints of works from Manet to Motherwell. Frame a few of these instead of plastering the walls with confusing flowered or plaid paper. Beautiful artwork is far more pleasing to the eye than clowns or hundreds of daisies.

When your child reaches the point where he thinks it's more fun to write on the wall than on a piece of paper, he'll be happy if one wall (or part of it) is covered with blackboard. Or buy a green chalkboard and have a carpenter cut out tree shapes to hang on the wall. A wall is also the greatest place to display kids' artwork and compositions. Tack board is available in all colors and can easily be put up. Homosote can be purchased in any lumberyard, then painted or covered in a natural burlap to serve the same purpose. Another, simpler solution is to hang butcher paper on one wall and let your child create. The paper comes down in a jiffy, and another piece can be put up for the next masterpiece.

What you do with the other important fixed architectural element in a child's room—windows—will depend on your aesthetics. Some people love curtains; others, venetians, shades, or shutters. There are endless styles, materials, and colors to choose from. The key consideration to keep in mind is that a window treatment should provide good lighting and air control. What kids really want is to be able to see out the window; they're not too concerned about what's around it.

Curtains often are too fussy for a child's room. Besides, they are terrible dust collectors, frequently having to be removed, cleaned, and maintained. By the same token, shutters, though attractive, are a nuisance—especially since you'll be the one doing all the opening and closing.

Room-darkening shades are inexpensive and functional. They darken the room totally when you want and let in lots of air and light when pulled up. Since children often wake up whenever any light comes in, this room-darkening feature is important to parents who prefer that their children sleep later than 6:00 A.M.

Vinyl-coated shades can be wiped down with a sponge and are weather-resistant. One good-looking vinyl shade features tiny pinholes, which, while they allow in more light than do opaque shades, add a decorative touch. For the energy-conscious, cloth shades with silver backings are especially practical. They act as insulators during the winter and heat reflectors in the summertime.

Venetian blinds give the best ventilation and light control. Modern thin-slatted Riviera aluminum blinds come in a rainbow of colors. You can even order them with more than one color, such as shades of blue from the lightest all the way up to deep navy. Slatted wood blinds with beveled edges prevent direct sunlight from entering the room but let air in. They're easy to maintain, inexpensive, and nice for a teenager's room.

Vertical blinds control air and light efficiently and, besides the thin-slatted Rivieras, are one of the best-looking window treatments you can install. However, they do not hold up well if abused, which is definitely an important consideration in a child's room. In addition, if you choose blinds, make certain that cords are inaccessible to those kids who love to grab everything in sight. The choice is yours.

5. More dramatic and visually exciting than draperies, vertical blinds are versatile and functional, offering excellent light, glare, and ventilation control. Side cords permit you to slant them at many angles.

Verticals are attached with either top or top and bottom tracks, depending on the installation and materials. They must be operated carefully, however, because they tend to go off the track if abused. We don't recommend verticals for youngsters, who like to tug on everything they see; wait until your child is eight or nine and understands how they work.

Vertical blinds are available in a wide choice of colors, finishes, and materials. The ones shown here are white PVC rigid plastic. The area covered is 83⅞ inches high by 118⅜ inches wide. Price: $260 installed.

LouverDrape Inc.: 1100 Colorado Avenue, Santa Monica, California 90401 Prices vary according to size

6. If your child doesn't mind some light entering the room at night, this is the shade to get. It's a glass fabric double-coated with white vinyl, and has lots of tiny perforations resembling pin pricks. Prettier than a plain white shade, it lets rays of light enter through the holes so the room won't be totally darkened. This shade is tough, durable and scrubbable, and would look handsome in any environment.

Holland Shade Co., Inc.: 306 East 61 Street, New York, New York 10021 $35—3 foot by 5 foot shade

7. Pirelli rubber flooring from Italy is often used in high traffic areas because of its easy maintenance qualities, durability, and wonderful looks. One Boston subway station had it installed twelve years ago, and it still looks like new.

Many designers and architects are recommending Pirelli for the home. After all, if it lasts at least twelve years when thousands are walking over it, think how long it will last in a child's room.

Comfortable to walk on and great for noise reduction, tiles come 20 or 40 inches square. There are a few styles, including ribbed and smooth, but the well-known studded look is most popular. Two thicknesses are available, low or high profile; but the low will certainly suffice at home. Pirelli is offered in a choice of twenty-seven colors. It is easy to clean with ammonia and water and can even be used as a wall covering.

Jason Industrial, Inc.: P.O. Box 365, 340 Kaplan Drive, Fairfield, New Jersey 07006 $2.20/square foot—black; $2.50/square foot—colors (low-profile studded) $2.45/square foot—black; $2.75/square foot—colors (high-profile studded)

Storage

Kids by nature are messy little creatures who grow to realize that chaos isn't convenient. Four boxes of crayons, seventeen coloring books, and fifty-five toys are great, until the crayons get lost under the bed, the books ripped, and the toys broken. But if there's a place for everything, everything will be in its place—unless the place is the wrong place.

Someone a long time ago thought dressers were neat ways to store things. Everything is shoved into a drawer and no one has to see what's happening inside. Drawers aren't convenient, though, and kids enjoy convenience. Did you ever see a child try to find a favorite book when it was buried under masses of other things in some dresser drawer? He starts tossing everything out until he gets what he wants. In the process, a few things manage to get broken, leaving a frustrated child.

In short, dressers and closets may be aesthetically pleasing to a parent, but if they're not convenient for a child, nothing will get put away. Screaming won't help. "Besides, most dressers are unsafe for little children since the drawers can easily fall on top of them," says Nancy Rambusch, director of the Caedmon School in New York.

Children like to put their possessions in places they can see. Open places—cubbies, cubes, bins, trays, totes, baskets, shelves. That way, they know where everything is and have more control over what they own . . . more sense of pride. A child should be able to think: Yesterday I found my crayons there and I'll find them there today. Children should be able to put aside what they're not using so they can handle what they are using.

Items should be stored so they are clearly distinguished from adjacent items: crayons in one bin; paintbrushes in another. Montessori started this concept when she said everything that goes together should go on a tray. Just pull out the right tray and you've got what you want. Trays provide control, permitting items to be organized so there's space around them. Things stored in this way are easy to find and easy to put back. This can work with clothes, too. Most little kids' garments fold, so there's no reason why sweaters, skirts, and pants can't be put away out in the open—on shelves or in cubes. They can even be organized by color: red shirts in one cube, blue pants in another. Your child won't have to start searching for his best T-shirt and might like putting it away in the first place. There's a set of see-through lucite drawers that would work well for this type of storage.

1. Fifty-eight inches high, 28 inches wide, and 20 inches deep, this metal trolley holds a louvered panel which in turn holds green, blue, red, and yellow plastic containers of various sizes on both sides. Kids can easily place the bins wherever they want and create interesting patterns. The largest measures 6 by 12½ by 20 inches.

Storage Concepts Group: 892 Broad Street, Newark, New Jersey 07102 $300 to $350, depending on number of bins and sizes used

Just like grown-ups, kids own little and big things, and little storage spaces are nice for little items, big for big items. Providing the right size space also tends to increase the specialness of what's being stored. Having a special cubby for crayons is much better than putting them together with lots of giant toys, which makes them hard to find. Cubbies are especially wonderful because they're child-size and more attractive to kids since they don't look like normal bulky pieces of furniture. Children who have cubbies no longer have the excuse that they can't reach the closet shelves.

Of course, not everything works best if stored in an open space, even if that's what kids prefer. While open-space storage is good during a child's first eight years, closed storage plays a bigger part later on, once the child has developed a sense of order.

Closed storage doesn't have to be a dresser even then. One twelve-year-old who has a collection of a hundred assorted balls was running out of space in which to store them. "I was constantly asking him to get them out of the way," his father says. "He finally decided he wanted file cabinets. I thought the idea was a little strange, but now he has two big cabinets, each marked 'Balls.' And he always puts the balls away."

"Parents visualize things a lot differently than children do. We fill up space with lots of furniture and then put the users [kids] into the space, and

2. A 15-foot expanse of lockers in varying configurations satisfies nearly all this youngster's storage needs. Here the double-door unit, 60 inches wide by 28 inches deep, with center shelf, is ideal for housing an elaborate stereo set. Two other units available consist of six lockers each. One configuration is vertical and measures 12 inches wide by 15 inches high by 21 inches deep; the other is horizontal at 18 inches wide by 10 inches high by 21 inches deep. The knockdown modules can be grouped and topped with a slab of butcher block or laminated to create a unified storage system.

These lockers are available through industrial sources but generally are listed under WOODWORKING BENCH STORAGE in the manufacturers' catalogs.

This setup is from Lyon Metal Products, which sells the units in standard gray and also offers a choice of fifteen custom colors for an additional charge.

Lyon Metal Products, Inc.: P.O. Box 671, Aurora, Illinois 60507 $230—double-door unit; $245—six-locker unit

often they don't feel comfortable with what we've provided," says Larry Malloy of Educational Facilities Labs.

Let your children decide what they want, even if it's a gray file cabinet for their tennis balls. "It should be easy to put things away," thinks Dr. Lee Salk, well-known child psychologist. Everything should be available at a correct height for seeing and reaching—everything displayed to encourage use. Put high shelves in a child's room and he'll use only what's on the bottom shelf. Nancy Rambusch says you can determine "storage zones" by having your child stand up and raise his hand. That's the highest his possessions should go.

You can encourage a child to put everything in place if you provide the proper resources. The idea is to give your child, four or fourteen, the responsibility of deciding where to store his goods. "You need to set up an attitude about order. Say: 'Here are a lot of things that have to be put away. You determine where you want them to go.' Don't just say: 'Clean up,'" advises Edith Axelson of the Rusk Institute.

In this chapter we are offering a multitude of storage systems, open and closed. Storage space that stays put; storage that moves on wheels. Storage units made of plastic, metal, wood, even net fabric. Round storage pieces and square ones. Big units and little. Not every piece will make sense in your home, of course. A rolling block cart may be great, but you may not have the room for it.

Many of the pieces will work for you as well as for the kids. You'll want places to put diapers, pins, ointments, and the other accessories of infanthood. Later on, they can hold the child's own equipment. Stacking boxes and cubes can be placed in different configurations and their tops used as work surfaces. Units that feature horizontal and vertical shelves for books and records plus cubes and drawers are excellent because they allow storage of many different items, each in its distinct area. Such units are particularly appealing to people who have limited space and not enough room for separate cubes, shelves, and drawers.

Shelves whose heights can be adjusted make more sense than fixed shelves because they can grow with the child. Shelving units on casters can operate as room dividers. It's a good idea to place a few small shelves right next to a child's bed. That way, she can have a book within arm's reach if she isn't sleepy and wants to read a bit.

Big bins are wonderful for big toys. Items stored in them should be of a similar kind, otherwise the material at the bottom won't get used. If the bin is on wheels, it can be transported easily from one play area to another. Kids love almost anything on wheels since they want to move all the time. "Wheels add another dimension," says Edith Axelson.

Take a careful look at your child's room and all his possessions. Give him the places to put them away—and cross your fingers.

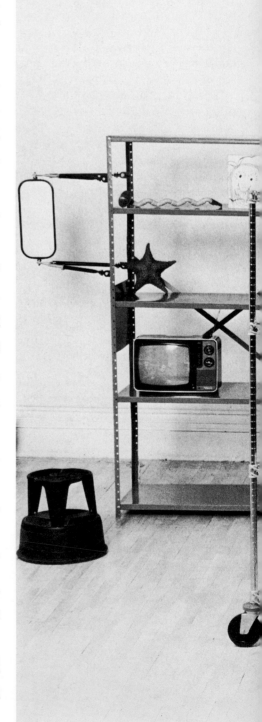

3

4

5

3. Steel-frame cabinets house crystal styrene see-through drawers to make storage units for lots of small things. A number of basic configurations are available with different-size drawers, ranging from a heavy-duty steel nine-drawer unit to a fifty-drawer lighter-weight system. Units can be mounted on the wall or stacked together. Most of them feature an unbreakable carrying handle so kids can take their miniature cars to a friend's. The nine-drawer unit, designed for industrial purposes, is 11 inches deep; the fifty-drawer system is 6 inches deep.

Akro-Mils: P.O. Box 989, Akron, Ohio 44309 $31—fifty drawers; $17—nine drawers

4. Some of these little plastic boxes have hinged transparent covers; some opaque covers. Others have lots of tiny compartments. All of them come in delicious colors and look lovely sitting on desks.

Wings Over the World Corp.: 225 Fifth Avenue, New York, New York 10010 $7—with compartments; $5—without

5. Resembling a workman's tool box, this little tote for kids can carry snacks to their room or toys to a friend's. It's made of orange heavy-duty plastic and is used in schools to carry group materials. Comes with a handle and measures 14 by 8¾ by 4½ inches.

Didax, Inc.: P.O. Box 2258, Peabody, Massachusetts 01960 $13

6. Little shelves can go up almost anywhere. The triangular-shaped trio would be convenient near a child's bed so she could reach over and grab a book before going to sleep. The high-grade plastic can be painted any color or left white; 6 inches by 6 inches by 11¾, 17¾, and 23¾ inches.

Beylerian, Ltd.: 305 East 63 Street, New York, New York 10022   **$14, $18, and $22**

7. Help set up a mini art studio for your young Picasso with these stainless-steel troughs. Designed to hold bar bottles in hotels and restaurants, they would look neat hanging on the wall next to an easel and filled with paint supplies. They come in 2-, 3-, or 4-foot lengths, with keyholes or straphangers. Brushes and paper can sit in one, paints in another.

Supreme Metal Fabricators, Inc.: 790 Summa Avenue, Westbury, New York 11590   **$24**—2-foot length; **$34**—3 feet; **$44**—4 feet

8. Nowadays, what teenager doesn't have a growing collection of cassette tapes? Help him find his favorite recording by providing storage carousels. One see-through unit can hold 25 tapes. Available with blue, orange, or yellow bases and tops.

Smith Systems: Box 3515, St. Paul, Minnesota 55165   **$19**—each

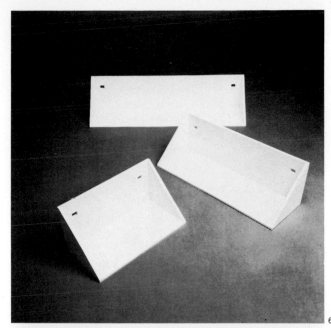

6

7

8

9

10

9. This chest is styled from many contrasting pieces of white oak and measures 19 by 34 by 16 inches. Roomy enough for all the trappings of childhood—and later—, it has an optional lift-out tray.

Charles Webb: 28 Church Street, Cambridge, Massachusetts 02138 $150; $45—tray

10. Blocks are basics in any child's environment, so a block cart could be one of the most welcome ways to set things straight when building time is done. Constructed of solid maple, this one glides on 2-inch heavy-duty casters and will hold little bodies when they want to play train. Measures 12 by 24 by 15 inches high, with a shelf that slopes to the rear.

Community Playthings: Rifton, New York 12471 $79.50 —cart with 85 blocks; $32.50—cart alone

11. A domed 15-gallon waste receptacle styled in shiny chrome or white can take the place of four little baskets, which often get overloaded and unsightly. Kids will love to swing the top and may even throw things into the container instead of on the floor. It looks like sculpture, comes with a plastic liner, and receives dirty laundry, too. Stands 36 inches high.

United Metal Receptacle: Fourteenth and Laurel Streets, Pottsville, Pennsylvania 17901 $143—chrome; $60—white

12. A simple white all-plastic step-on container gets dirty disposable or cloth diapers out of the way. The inside pail lifts out easily. Holds eighteen quarts and stands 15½ inches high. It can be sanitized with steam and washes in a jiffy.

Rubbermaid Commercial Products, Inc.: 3124 Valley Avenue, Winchester; Virginia 22601 $28

13. Sometimes it's fun to find inexpensive items designed for one purpose and use them for another. These simple, white rubber wastebaskets can be filled to the brim with toys and placed against a wall—a ready-made storage setup that costs only pennies. A bunch of them can be labeled T O Y S. These, from Rubbermaid, measure 14½ by 8¼ by 15 inches high.

Rubbermaid: 1147 Akron Road, Wooster, Ohio 44691 $4

14. This beautiful, classic-looking wastebasket doesn't have to be hidden under the desk. Made of heavy-duty steel with baked-enamel finish in black, putty, brown, red, white, or blue, it's 15 inches high with a 10-inch diameter.

Smokador Products Division: 470 West First Avenue, Roselle, New Jersey 07203 $16

11

13

12

14

15. A bright red rolling cart would make a colorful, practical addition to a child's room. Made of heavy-duty steel, it will support anything from a TV to a set of toy trains. This cart rolls on 3-inch ball-bearing casters with rubber treads. Comes with top and bottom shelves and one drawer with padlock so your ten-year-old can keep something private. A center shelf and additional drawers can be purchased. Measures 29 inches wide by 18 inches deep and 34 inches high.

Shure Manufacturing Corp.: 1601 South Hanley Road, St. Louis, Missouri 63144 **$70**

16. Set up a TV or stereo system on this rolling steel utility cart. The top measures 18 by 30 inches and will accommodate most portable TVs. Stands 26 inches high, a good viewing height. Four-inch ball-bearing swivel casters let you roll it easily, even when there are 300 pounds of equipment on top. The bottom shelf can hold lots of records. Neutral baked-enamel finish with heavy-ribbed rubber pad top. Comes with an optional electrical assembly and 20-foot power cord in case you want to use the table as a home movie projector stand.

The Advance Products Co.: 1101 East Central, P.O. Box 2178, Wichita, Kansas 67214 **$70; $12**—20-foot power cord

17. Books, records, and cassettes can roll from room to room on this solid steel four-shelf resource center. Casters are 4 inches; two come with brakes. The unit is 36 inches wide and 46 or 64 inches high. Shelves are 8, 10, or 12 inches deep. An optional sloped display shelf is available for showing off favorite books or albums.

Smith System: P.O. Box 3515, St. Paul, Minnesota 55165 $270—46-inch resource center with 12-inch shelves; $20—display shelf

18. The Utility Art Cart can take on diapers to start; crayons, coloring books, and toys a little later on; school supplies, books, even clothes during the next stage; and, finally, bar accessories when the children are grown. It's made of solid maple for durability and looks good enough to bring into the dining room. Measures 20 by 28 inches inside and stands 30 inches tall on 2-inch diameter casters. Includes four tote boxes.

Community Playthings: Rifton, New York 12471 $75

17

18

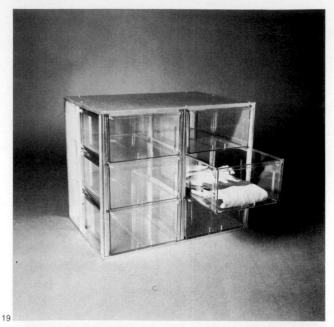

19.

19. If you've ever spent fifteen minutes looking for your child's favorite stuffed animal or the blue pajamas Aunt Geri bought him, you might like these clear plastic see-through storage drawers. They interlock and can be stacked to any height and tucked away in the closet. Set them up right in view—they'll look pretty filled with all the colorful clothes and toys of childhood. Measuring 15½ inches long, 10 inches wide, and 6 inches deep, each drawer comes with a cover. Handy folks can build a wood cabinet for the drawers and create an inexpensive permanent storage system. An optional aluminum-clad steel cabinet holds six drawers. You can also get a kick-base that elevates the drawers so they won't get scratched when you're vacuuming.

Result Manufacturing: 712 Stewart Avenue, Garden City, New York 11530 $80—cabinet with six drawers; $10—kickbase

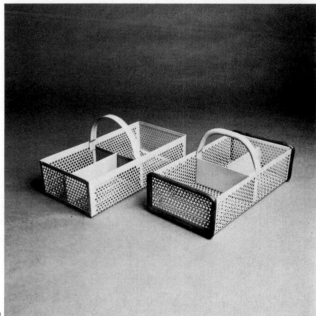

20.

20. You might like these maid's baskets for your baby supplies. Made of perforated steel, each features a trio of compartments. Ointments can go in one area, cotton in another, and powder in the third. One tote has bumpers on both sides and a tubular handle; the other has rubber feet to prevent scratches to furniture. Available in gray or blue. Custom-ordered colors available with bulk purchase.

Harloff Manufacturing Co.: 750 Garden of Gods Road, Colorado Springs, Colorado 80907 $14—with rubber feet; $16—with bumpers

21.

21. Montessori believed everything should be stored on trays—but baskets can serve just as well. Put anything you want inside these sturdy chromed metal wire baskets and set them on top of a desk or stack them on shelves. The low one measures 18 inches by 26 inches by 2 inches high and was actually designed to hold donuts. The utility model is 18 inches by 24 inches by 10 inches.

Metropolitan Wire Corp.: George Street and North Washington Avenue, Wilkes-Barre, Pennsylvania 19705 $37—utility; $13—donut

22. Another way to encourage clean ups: the same receptacle used on city streets can come indoors. Standing two feet high, it's made of heavy-duty perforated steel and enamel-coated in red, white, and blue, solid black, or pencil orange. A "Don't Be a Litter Bug" sign is optional, but fun. Holds 10 gallons of garbage, and is also sufficiently weighted to hold tall toys such as bats, hockey sticks, skis, even umbrellas.

United Metal Receptacle: Fourteenth and Laurel Streets, Pottsville, Pennsylvania 17901 $49—red, white, and blue; $46—solids

23. Four roomy basket drawers slide in and out of a simple frame to display clearly what's being stored. The Elfa basket drawer system from Sweden can travel from bath to playroom, sit on top of a desk, or rest on the closet floor. A bunch of systems will easily take the place of a dresser.

Baskets are made of welded steel wire and coated with a special plastic that supposedly won't peel. The rack is brown metal. Available in three heights: 17½ inches, 29½ inches (shown), and 41 inches; four widths: 10 inches to 21¾ inches. All units are 21½ inches deep. Drawers are available from 3⅜ inches to 15¼ inches high.

Scan Plast Industries, Inc.: 1 Industrial Drive, Rutherford, New Jersey 07070 $70—29½ inches high, 17¾ inches wide; three 7½-inch drawers, one 3⅜-inch drawer $15—four heavy-duty casters

22

23

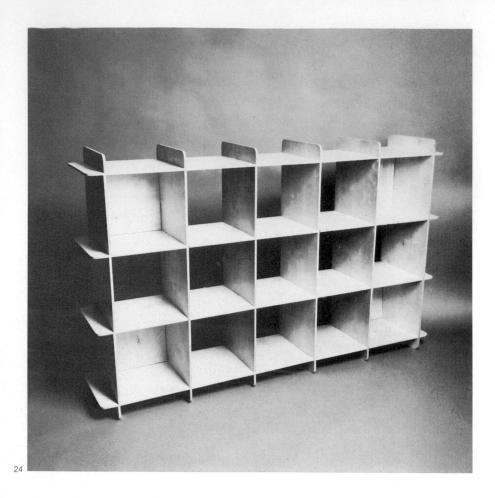

24.

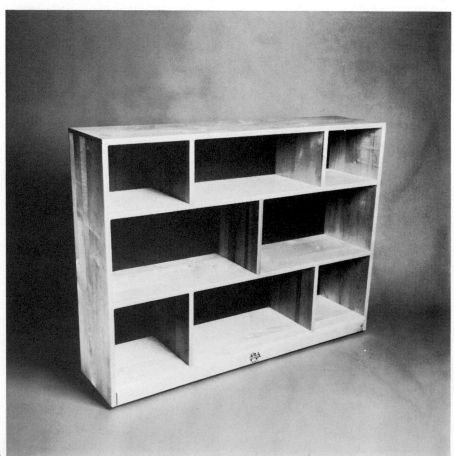

25.

24. Freestanding storage units, good for items of odd sizes and shapes, work best against a wall but can also be used as room dividers. Simply designed and made of Baltic birch with a satin clear finish, this one features fifteen spacious cubbies. Overall dimensions are 60 inches wide by 38 inches high by 12 inches deep. The top ledge can also hold goodies.

PlayLearn Products Division, PCA Industries, Inc.: 2298 Grisson Drive, St. Louis, Missouri 63144 **$110**

25. Store blocks and books on a set of solid maple shelves. Rolls on 2-inch heavy-duty casters so the kids can easily move their materials about. This also works nicely as a room divider, with its pegboard back. Measures 48 inches long, 36 inches high, and 11½ inches deep.

Community Playthings: Rifton, New York 12471 **$98**

26. Harriet Ziefert has two sons, six and eleven, who have baseball gloves, sneakers, tennis rackets, balls, bats, sweat shirts, and other things Harriet can't even recall. Luckily, Harriet also has a big house but unluckily, she doesn't have much storage space. So this mother, with all these kid possessions and her limited storage facilities, decided to install an entire wall of Lyon Metal's gym lockers—right in her big kitchen.

"I was tired of everything cluttering up the front hall, yet I still wanted it all to be stored downstairs. It's more convenient to have sporting equipment ready to grab as you're leaving the house than to store it in an upstairs bedroom," Harriet says.

Why lockers? "I chose them because they allow a great deal of flexibility. Some are tall, for tennis rackets and coats, others are small, for sneakers and balls." The basic configuration measures 72 inches by 72 inches by 12 inches and has 12 footlockers, two 72-inch lockers and four 36-inch units.

26

27. This reasonably priced commercial-type shelving is made of heavy-gauge steel and can hold up to two hundred pounds per shelf. Each shelf can be adjusted at 1½–inch increments and is supported by one-piece compression clips that fit into the posts. Easy to assemble, the basic five-shelf unit is freestanding and can take on additional structures. Steel side panels and back cross braces provide strength and rigidity. Gray baked-on enamel. Four sizes: 36 inches by 12 inches by 6 feet, 36 by 12 by 7 feet, 36 by 18 by 6 feet, and 36 by 18 by 7 feet. Fill them with toys, games, stereos, or anything you need a place for. The Atlas shelves can even be mounted upside down, forming a tray to hold rolling items.

Hallowell Division, Standard Pressed Steel Co.: Township Line Road, Hatfield, Pennsylvania 19440 $36, $39, $47, and $49

28. Swing it open and it's a big storage cabinet with twenty cubbies and five large shelves. Swing it closed and roll it against the wall, out of the way, or make it a room divider. Constructed of natural-finish wood with piano-type hinges for strength and durability. Roomy plastic hold-all trays will indeed hold all—clothes, coloring books, paint supplies, blocks, boats. And they're see-through, so your child will know where everything is at a glance. The unit also locks. Each side measures 48 inches long, 13 inches deep, and 30 inches high.

Childcraft Education Corp.: 20 Kilmer Road, Edison, New Jersey 08817 $225

29. Too often we don't use valuable wall space intelligently. Since it's there, why waste it? As your family grows larger and your quarters seem to get smaller, try to make the walls work. Shelves are the most obvious storage systems, but there is a multitude of other solutions. Akrobins is one: A heavy-duty louvered steel panel is mounted on a wall or inside a cabinet. Once the panel is up, unbreakable polypropylene bins are hooked into place, ready for use.

The red, yellow, and blue bins come in five sizes and can be purchased separately, depending on your needs. They can also be used alone. The bigger bins, measuring 14¾ by 16½ by 7 inches, are ideal for shoes; the tinier ones, 5⅜ by 4⅛ by 3 inches, hold lots of odds and ends. Panels are each 19 inches high and 35¾ inches wide, designed to lap together vertically to form units as high as 73 inches. Akrobins were originally conceived for industrial use, but you may find them colorful and practical at home.

Akro Mils. P.O. Box 989, Akron, Ohio 44309 $14—panel; $7—big bins; $.60—small bins

30. Seven injection-molded plastic bins sit in a row along a 44-inch steel wall rail. Each bin measures 5 inches high by 9 inches deep by 6 inches wide, and is roomy enough to hold art supplies, small toys, even cosmetics or jewelry.

The rail has a gray stove-enamel finish and the hook-on bins are available in red or yellow. The system is easy to put up with a few screws and makes a clean-looking, convenient storage rack.

Storage Concepts Group: 892 Broad Street, Newark, New Jersey 07102 $30—rail; $2.50—each bin

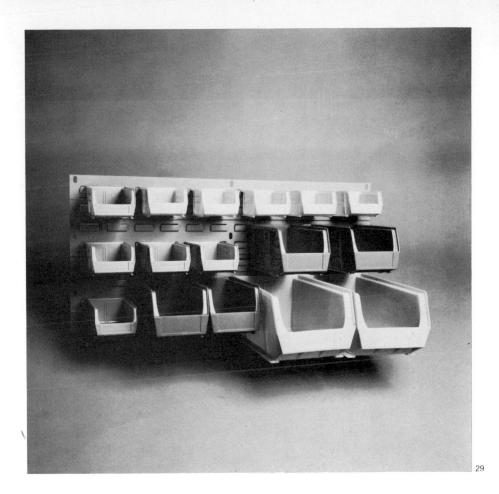

29

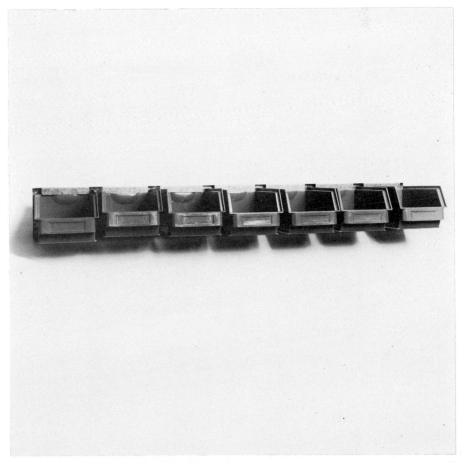

30

31

31. An inexpensive freestanding open-shelf system that can grow as your child accumulates possessions. Shelves are made of ponderosa pine and can hold lots of weight, including a big stereo or tape system. They have steel end channels that rest firmly on steel pins. Uprights are hemlock. The only tool you'll need to put together the system is a screwdriver. The basic unit stands 72 inches high and 36 inches wide. Shelves come 12, 15, or 18 inches deep.

Lundia, Myers Industries, Inc.: 600 Capitol Way, Jacksonville, Illinois 62650 $60.00—four 15-inch shelves; $50.00—add-on unit; $16.50—extra shelves

32. A basic unit of this library system is 78 inches high, 10 inches deep, and 36 inches wide, with six shelves. The frame of the unit is beige; the shelves are dashing in matte black, but also come in orange, blue, green, red, neutral, and seven other colors. Place them against an entire wall to house your child's book and toy collection. Double-face units are also available; they make attractive freestanding room dividers. There is a choice of two other heights: 42 inches (three shelves) and 68 inches (five shelves). The depth of the shelves ranges from 7 inches to 11 inches. Shown here is a basic six-shelf system with an add-on unit. Measures 72 inches wide.

Republic Steel Industrial Products Division: 1038 Belden Avenue N.E., Canton, Ohio 44705 $300

32

33. Designed for industrial use and heavy-duty operations in hospitals, restaurants, and even greenhouses, this mobile shelf truck can function just as efficiently at home. Four chrome-plated steel shelves can be adjusted at 1-inch increments over the entire height of the posts. Stacks of sweaters or rows of little shoes would look colorful sitting against the cool steel, and would get plenty of air since the shelves are open. Add gray plastic tote boxes or wire utility baskets when you need to contain things. The system rolls easily on rubber wheels and would work as a room divider. Measures 18 inches by 60 inches by 72 inches; other sizes available.

Metropolitan Wire Corp.: George Street and North Washington Avenue, Wilkes-Barre, Pennsylvania 18705 $297

34. Gray steel industrial shelving has always stood up well in factories. Now it's finding its way into the home, gussied up with a coat of rust, white, yellow, or chocolate-brown paint for those who like the industrial look but don't want to go all the way. Constructed of lighter-gauge steel than commercial shelving, this home unit will still stand up to lots of weight. Shelves are 12 inches deep and 30 inches wide. Three-, five-, or six-shelf units are available, with 31-, 60-, and 73-inch heights. Plastic floor protectors guard against scratches.

The company also manufactures a complete line of heavier-gauge commercial pieces available in any color.

Fort Steuben Metal Products Co.: Fort Steuben Road, Weirton, West Virginia 26062 $9.95—three-shelf unit; $17.95—five-shelf unit; $23.95—six-shelf unit

33

34

35. Thirty-two roomy metal wire baskets sit in a handsome blue steel locker rack, ready to serve as a storage unit for anything you like. And anything would look good in it—towels, toys, sweaters, shirts—since all the colors would show through. The one shown here is 51⅜ inches wide, 77½ inches high, and 13⅜ inches deep. A number of other widths is available, but all units stand 77½ inches high. Each basket is 12 inches wide by 13 inches deep by 8 inches high. The rack is available in eighteen other colors.

Republic Steel, Industrial Products Division: 1038 Belden Avenue N.E., Canton, Ohio 44705 **$415**

36. Everyone remembers racing to the locker room after gym class, showering, and then standing in front of her own special locker to change. The locker became a little home for all our gear— sneakers, gym suit, soap, brushes, and towels. Well, lockers make as much sense at home as they do in school. And they don't have to be gym-room gray either. A row of them painted in bold bright blue, red, or yellow can liven up any environment.

Lockers can hold almost anything. There are hooks for coats or shirts, enough height for stacks of sweaters, and floor space for sneakers and shoes. Constructed of heavy-gauge steel, the ones shown here have kickproof handles and doors that close silently, so you won't hear slamming every time a kid wants his baseball bat. Locker systems come in a variety of widths, depths, and heights— these are 72 inches high. You might consider a variety of configurations (box, single- or double-tier) to suit your individual storage needs.

Republic Steel Industrial Products Division: 1038 Belden Avenue N.E., Canton, Ohio 44705 **$260**

35b

36

37.

Stacking baskets have a variety of uses; they're the solution for organizing things that should be easy to find and reach. These are made of durable high-grade molded plastic in red, yellow, green, or white. There's no end to how many you can stack. Each basket measures 13⅛ by 20½ by 8⅞ inches. A set of four casters is also available.

Beylerian, Ltd.: 305 East 63 Street, New York, New York 10022 $6—each basket; $5—set of four casters.

38.

Big and sturdy, this all-metal hamper will work just fine for toys at home. The sheet steel is perforated so kids can spot the exact location of their favorite doll. When the toys are all out, the hamper is big enough to hold one or two tots who want to play inside. Measuring 41 inches long, 25 inches wide and 24 inches deep, it has 10-inch wheels—two rigid and two that swivel—and semi-pneumatic tires. Finish is gleaming white enamel for a clean look.

Harloff Manufacturing Co.: 750 Garden of Gods Road, Colorado Springs, Colorado 80907 $211

39.

Many schools use the cart, far right, because it's spacious, mobile, and can be locked. Made of solid birch plywood and finished with urethane paint, it rolls on four casters. There's one shelf inside. The unit is 29 inches high by 30 inches wide and 20 inches deep.

Roomy plastic tote trays sit neatly in the enclosed nylon-coated steel wire rack at left. Convenient pieces of storage gear to place near work or play surfaces, these racks can hold eight or twelve trays. Each tray measures 4 by 13½ by 18 inches. The optional outer container of domestic birch plywood, comes in a choice of eight colors ranging from the primaries to white, beige, and brown.

Cameron-McIndoo U.S.A.: North Bennington, Vermont 05257 $300—mobile cart; $98—rack with eight totes; $140—outer container

40a

40b

40. This simple three-drawer fir wood dresser can work in any decor you've chosen for the nursery. Covered in white, brown, yellow, or red lead-free plastic paint, it is 20½ inches wide, 21½ inches deep, and 25½ inches high, including a 4-inch base. Dressers can be stacked next to or on top of one another for people with lots of things to store. Optional baby changing table with vinyl cover on top features a shelf for towels or diapers. Measuring 22 inches wide, 14¾ inches high, and 23 inches deep, the table conveniently turns into a seat for mother.

Scandinavian Design: 117 East 57 Street, New York, New York 10022 $147—Muurame chest; $82—changing table

41a

41b

41. Playful-looking bands of red, blue, yellow, and green accent the four extra-large drawers on this combination dresser/chest. Styled in maple with a natural finish, the contemporary unit can brighten up a baby's or teenager's room. The flip-top dressing area makes a convenient infant changing table—and, later on, a vanity for your daughter. A white plastic pad with safety strap is included. Dresser measures 42½ inches high by 35 1/32 inches wide by 16 9/16 inches deep.

Child Craft: P.O. Box 444, Salem, Indiana 47167 $200

42

42. An eighteen-drawer tray storage unit would work well next to a worktable. Constructed of 5/8-inch veneered beechwood with a light oak finish, it has large, easy-to-open drawers. Inside dimensions are 24½ inches high by 33¼ inches wide by 15½ inches deep. A six-drawer unit, 11¾ inches wide, is also available, which can be nestled under a worktable.

Childcraft Education Corp.: 20 Kilmer Road, Edison, New Jersey 08817 $200—eighteen-drawer unit; $100—six-drawer unit

43. Over a hundred record albums can find a home in this compact steel storage cabinet. The sides are white, the front metallic blue, and the fully adjustable shelf is yellow. There's a lock on the latching door for youngsters who don't want their brothers or sisters to take a favorite album. Stands 16¾ inches high. Several units can be stacked or bolted together side by side.

The Advance Products Co.: 1101 East Central, P.O. Box 2178, Wichita, Kansas 67214 $80

43

44

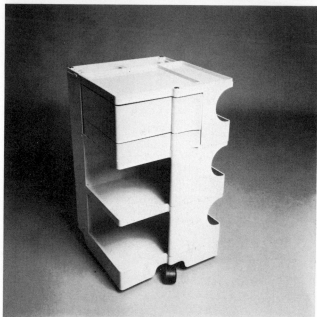

45

46

44. Molded plastic stacking chest system comes in three-, four-, or five-drawer multiples as well as single-drawer add-ons. Optional casters are handy. White or dark brown only. Each drawer measures 5½ inches high by 16½ square. Two units can form the base of a desk; one alone makes a side table.

Beylerian, Ltd.: 305 East 63 Street, New York, New York 10022 $17.50—one drawer; $55.00—three drawers; $70.00—four drawers; $85.00—five drawers

45. This is called the BoBy, and although it's expensive, it may just turn out to be your best friend when the children are growing. It will hold almost anything, and it's mounted on casters so you can roll it to your side anywhere at home. There are several versions. This one is made up of three stacking modules and has two swing-out trays, five open compartments, and special inserts for tall items. For a little extra, you can get a lock for the top tray. The BoBy is styled in plastic and comes in white, yellow, red, black, brown, green, or orange. Width and depth are 17 inches; height is 29 inches with three modules and 21 inches with 2 modules.

Inter/Graph, Ltd.: 979 Third Avenue, New York, New York 10022 $180—29-inch; $156—21-inch

46. An industrial toter, this model has three locking drawers and glides on 4-inch casters. Drawers measure 20 inches wide by 20 inches deep by 6 inches high. Comes in bright red baked enamel on steel. Tucks under Shure's Big Red workbench for additional drawer space.

Shure Manufacturing Corp.: 1601 South Hanley Road, St. Louis, Missouri 63144 $186

47a. Everyone wants more storage space and mobile pedestals are the perfect way. One of a dozen great baked-enamel colors, from red to black, coat this steel unit. The top, also available in a wide color choice, is laminated, so it won't scratch or soil. The four-drawer locking unit shown here measures 27¾ inches high, 15⅞ inches wide, and 17½ inches deep. It also comes in 22- or 28-inch depths. Many combinations of file, box, and tray drawers are available, all with recessed drawer pulls. The pedestal comes with casters, permitting easy rolling under or next to a desk.

Designcraft: 111 Kero Road, Carlstadt, New Jersey 07072 $180

47b. This rolling tool chest will stand up to lots of abuse and still look as solid as the day it was manufactured. Classically simple with a gray baked-enamel finish, it's something to think about as a way of storing things. Drawers measure 21¾ inches wide by 20 inches deep by 6¾ inches high. Four or six units bolted together and placed on wheels make a handsome chest. Each drawer comes with a sliding tray and operates on ball-bearing rollers, so it won't be difficult for young people to get what they want.

Lyon Metal Products, Inc.: P.O. Box 671, Aurora, Illinois 60507 $212—four-drawer unit

48. These office file cabinets, available with 2-inch drawers, can be packed with all the small things that fill your child's life and make you wish you had more space. The cabinet can also double as a little night table. There are two sizes: a 13-inch-high 5-drawer unit for desk top or bedside, and a 29-inch-high 10-drawer unit for under-desk use. If you take two of the taller model, you can use them as the base of a desk, topped by a slab of wood or Formica. The cabinets come in white, yellow, or brown enameled steel with chromed handles.

Conran's: The Market at Citicorp Center, 160 East 54 Street, New York, New York 10022 (dealer); or F. C. Brown, Ltd.: Queens Road, Bisley, Surrey, England $58—five drawer unit; $99—ten-drawer unit (mfg.)

47a

47b

48

49a

49. No matter what kind of sport your child favors, chances are he's amassed a supply of balls. Now he can put them all together in nylon ball carriers and cart them to the playing field. These heavy-duty white knotless nylon carriers come in two sizes for small or big balls. There's a 1½-inch-square mesh for baseballs, tennis balls, or even laundry, and a 4-inch-square mesh for basketballs, footballs, and stuffed toys.

Jayfro Corp.: P.O. Box 400, Waterford, Connecticut 06385
$6—1½-inch mesh; $8—4-inch mesh

50. An all-purpose tote carrier can make it easier to transport bats, balls, toys, even laundry from one spot to the next. A compact sturdy steel and aluminum frame supports this expandable heavy-duty nylon net container. The see-through weave lets you or your child see what's inside at a glance. There are four non-scuff tires: two semi-pneumatic and two casters for easy mobility. Measures 3½ feet long by 2 feet wide by 3 feet high. Although this is a fairly expensive item, it will serve everyone in the family, and last at least until the youngest goes off to college.

Jayfro Corp.: P.O. Box 400, Waterford, Connecticut 06385 $100

49b

51. If you're tired of storing everything in cubes, it could be nice to switch to rounds. These circular units with doors are known as the Stacking Storage Things and can be piled as high as you like. They'll make good hiding places for all those towels or diapers. A two-unit multiple has a 12½-inch diameter and is 15¾ inches high. It comes in red, white, yellow, or dark brown plastic. Casters and trays are optional.

Beylerian, Ltd.: 305 East 63 Street, New York, New York 10022   **$52**

52. An open box and multicube with door can be used individually or together. The open piece is 15 by 15 by 9½ inches high; the cube is 15 by 15 by 15⅛ inches. White or brown high-grade plastic. Surround the closed unit with two open boxes, use two open pieces together, or build a big system.

Beylerian, Ltd.: 305 East 63 Street, New York, New York 10022   **$30**—cube with door; **$18**—open box

53. When the day is over and the playroom is strewn with toys and books, stash everything in a cube. These are plastic, stackable, and modeled like milk-box cartons with grids and side handle grips. When the toys come out, the cubes make great building blocks, step stools, and trains for creative-thinking kids. They come in a variety of bright colors and measure 15 inches.

Mack Molding. Arlington, Vermont 05250 **$10**

54. A pair of colorful storage cubes glides around on four smooth rolling casters. One's sunshine yellow, one rich red, and they each measure 9¾ inches high, 13¾ inches wide, and 9½ inches deep. Your child can separate them and ride around in the bottom half.

Childcraft Education Corp.: 20 Kilmer Road, Edison, New Jersey 08817 (dealer)
Baby Djörn, Björn Stign 119, Box 743 17107, Solna 7, Sweden **$20** (mfg.)

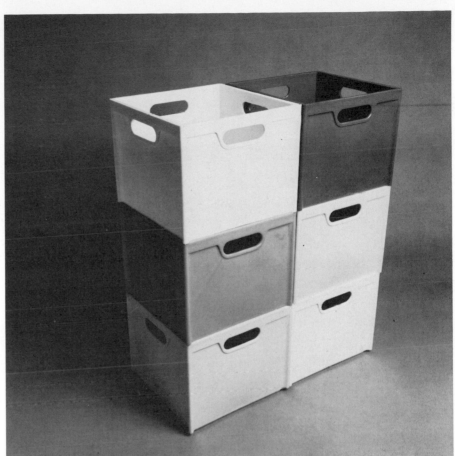

53

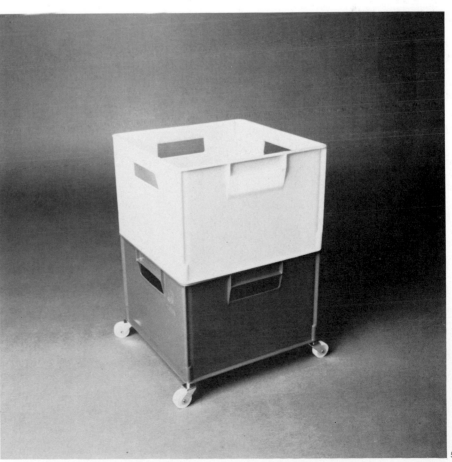

54

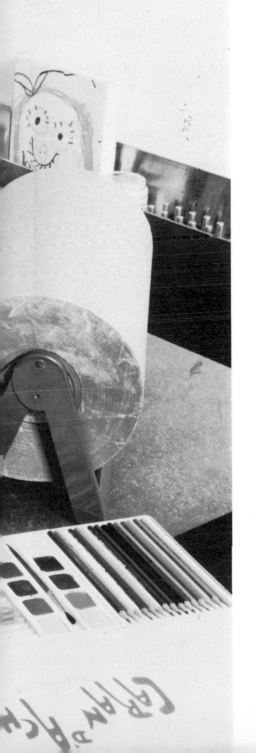

Surfaces
for Work & Play

One of the most wonderful things about children is their inability to distinguish between work and play. They work at play and play at work. Providing the right trappings keeps them in this happy play/work spirit. "Work doesn't have to be unpleasant and play can be more fun if they're done in the right environments with appropriate tools," claims Nancy Rambusch, director of New York City's Caedmon School. "If you want to teach your five-year-old to be a Harlem Globetrotter, don't hang the basketball hoop twelve feet from the ground; hang it at a height to which he can relate."

There are lots of ways to make your children happy at their activities, whether they're coloring, reading, eating, learning the multiplication tables, or putting together model airplanes. It simply helps to understand how a child relates to his environment. Too many parents do not remember what it was like to be three feet tall.

Little children love spaces and things they can

control. You may not feel it necessary to buy a small table and chairs, thinking your child can do almost anything at the kitchen table. But little people like child-size furniture since so many things around them are adult-size. "It's easier for them to be comfortable when their feet can reach the floor," notes Robin Berenstain, who runs a Denver day-care center. Providing children with furniture scaled to their height and capabilities will encourage them to act independently. They won't have to wait for you to clear off the dining room table when they want to start some activity.

Small tables, just like big ones, come in all shapes. Nancy Rambusch says that round surfaces, which invite group interaction, are good for social activities such as eating, meeting, and reading, while square tables are better for working.

Many creative activities, like painting, require larger spaces. A low table with a wide horizontal surface lets kids sit around it on the floor. Or you can cover a Ping-Pong table with vinyl, place a roll of drawing paper at one end, and let the child roll it out as his imagination unfolds. It's also nice to provide "work" spaces at different heights, since some activities are more comfortable done standing and others sitting. Different structures at various heights can also help define spheres of activity: in a bedroom, for instance, one area, with one surface, can be set aside for serious quiet work and another for active work.

There is a variety of wonderfully versatile tables that serve several functions and save space to boot. If you have limited space, this is cer-

1. The child's drawing corner on the preceding page is inexpensive, easy to set up, and will give your youngster much enjoyment.

First comes the clear, heavy-duty polycarbonate utility mat, used by office workers because it permits chairs to glide more easily over carpeting. Put it in a corner of the playroom where anyone can fingerpaint, color, and generally mess around right on top of it without getting the floor dirty. There are four sizes ranging from 36 by 48 inches to 60 by 72.

Then comes the drawing surface—and there's nothing quite so practical as plain brown paper when kids want to scribble and develop their artistic bents. The All-In-One paper cutter will keep your youngster constantly supplied. The steel frame can't warp or break and is practically impossible to damage. The double-edge tempered cutter has no threatening blade, just a sharp edge.

The All-In-One requires no assembly and has no loose parts. Just spread the base and it's ready to use. The cutter is provided with a mounting hole in each corner of the base, permitting installation on the top or underside of a table or strong wooden shelf, or on a strong wall or door. If you're not sure you have a sturdy enough mounting surface, simply sit the All-In-One on the floor.

The finish is gray baked-on enamel. Each roll measures 18 inches wide by 9 inches in diameter. Mounting instructions are included in the package.

The drawing corner is further equipped with Supreme Metal's stainless troughs for paints; Kulicke's frames for paintings; and a Luxo lamp.

Bulman Products Division, Rospatch Corp.: 1650 McReynolds Avenue N.W., Grand Rapids, Michigan 49504 $18

Rubbermaid Commercial Products, Inc.: Winchester, Virginia 22601 $35—36 inch by 48 inch utility mat; $89—60 inch by 72 inch mat

63

2. **Small scale . . . but mature lines.** This solid oak children's table and chair set lets the young ones eat, play, and work together, but still feel like they're important people. Table measures 26 inches long, 20 inches wide, and 22½ inches high, so it can stay in the kitchen—out of the way.

Georgia Chair Co.: P.O. Box 935, Gainesville, Georgia 30501 $80

tainly a preferable alternative to cramming three different tables into one small area. Tables don't have to just stand there; they can be adjusted, rolled around on wheels, collapsed, or hinged to the wall and folded down.

Adjustable tables grow with the child, so they'll make sense for a long time. One child we know has one that tilts. When it's flat, he can do his homework on it; when it's tilted, he uses it as a music stand. Tables on wheels can be transported easily from one room to another whenever a child wants to change her milieu. Collapsible tables are great space savers, as are the wall-mounted models that fold down from a hinge. When you buy a folding table, however, make sure that little hands can't get caught where the two pieces collapse. And check whether a young child can close the table himself. If he can, chances are it's not the one to buy.

Although it's important to provide work/play surfaces just as soon as children get off the floor, it's most important when they begin school. A child who becomes accustomed to doing homework on the living room floor will probably produce sloppy results. The floor goes on and on, and so will his penmanship. A desk begins and ends, providing a needed sense of confinement and limitation.

Desks with side walls create individual places to read, think, and work. They are great for younger children, who have to learn to be private in a social setting. These carrels work well when there are two children at home in the same room —one doing homework and the other playing. It has been found that children like a sense of enclosure when they are concentrating on a relatively quiet and passive activity. This enclosure defines a space and distinguishes it from adjoining areas where other activities are taking place.

There are also desk/chair combinations that are portable and ideal space savers. Or desks with file cabinet bases that provide big storage spaces for compositions and notebooks. A lap desk is another alternative, not for serious work that demands a great deal of attention but for lighter work, like coloring a map of Europe. "More children might work on a lap desk since they can use it on the floor or in bed," says Marion Pasnik of the New York City Board of Education. We are not showing a specific model here, but recommend instead that you make one out of a lightweight Masonite or wood board, with side panels or legs or use a bed tray.

Work and play aren't limited to horizontal surfaces. Blackboards, tack boards, and easels should be part of every child's environment, not just for school. They can encourage creativity at home as well. Marion Pasnik likes plain, ordinary blackboards on casters since they can be room dividers and space definers. She also thinks one wall of a child's room should be tack board "so the child can hang up anything he wants. You can get any color. Tan would be nice," she says.

Work and play surfaces should be easy to clean so you won't be yelling at your child if he forgets the paper and starts drawing on the table. An environment in which a young child can take care of his physical needs and independently embark on a variety of work or play activities fosters a sense of self-reliance, according to educators.

3. A convenient work or play environment is created from these three basic elements. The L & B white laminate table with cast-iron pedestal base comes with a removable divider so siblings can share the surface. The table top is 42 inches square. The all-steel mobile storage unit rolls on chrome casters and features a convenience drawer for pens, pencils, and small accessories; a storage drawer; and a big file drawer for notebooks and papers. Other drawer configurations are also available. Measures 15 inches wide by 18 inches deep by 24⅝ inches high. The painted acrylic enamel finish comes in black (shown here) or in nineteen other brilliant colors, including garnet, tobacco, orange, yellow, green, beige, and maize. The white Kevi chair completes the setting in style.

L& B Products Corp.: 3232 Lurting Avenue, Bronx, New York 10469 $90—base; $70—top (36 inches square)
Sunar Ltd. Steel Division: 1 Sunshine Avenue, Waterloo, Ontario, Canada $375—storage unit

4. Teenagers with lots of hobbies will enjoy this combination rolling tool chest and big work top. So will dad. The work surface comes in steel, pressed wood on steel, or laminated hardwood and measures 60 by 29 by 34 inches. Higher than standard-size desks, it can still function as one with the addition of an adjustable chair or stool. If a lower unit is desired, a 31-inch workbench is also available. There's one locking drawer. The matching chest rolls on 4-inch casters, measures 21¼ inches long by 20½ inches wide by 31 inches high, and has three locking drawers. When purchased with the 34-inch workbench, the chest nestles conveniently under it. Should you buy the 31-inch workbench, the chest will have to sit to one side. Both pieces are finished in cardinal red baked-on enamel.

Shure Manufacturing Co.: 1601 South Hanley Road, St. Louis, Missouri 63144 $113—workbench with steel top; $148—with pressed wood; $227—with laminated hardwood; $186—Tool Toter

3

4

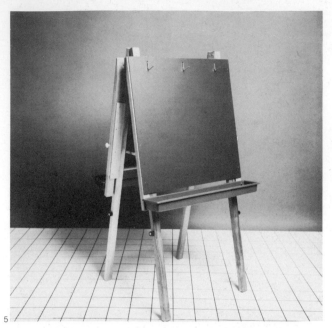

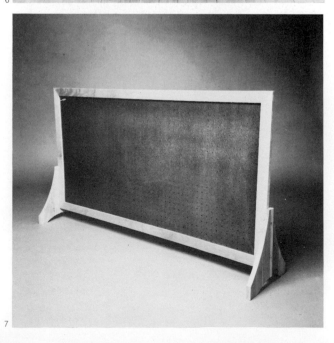

5. It's much easier to paint on an easel than on top of the kitchen table—and much less messy. A double easel lets two artists create at once and prevents arguing. Waterproof removable trays hold jars and brushes. Hardboard panels are 24 inches square with green chalkboard finish. Each side is adjustable to a 53-inch maximum height, and locking braces hold the easel rigidly when open. Three removable pegboard hooks come on top of each panel.

Community Playthings: Rifton, New York 12471 **$43**

6. Ping-Pong tables aren't just for playing Ping-Pong; they provide nice big horizontal work or play surfaces. Cover one with a piece of vinyl when your youngster wants to finger-paint. The playback Roll-a-Way is made of high-density particle board with 1-inch painted green steel legs and steel frame. One side can be flipped up like a backboard when the champion wants to practice. Flip the other side up to store the table against the wall, out of the way. Measures 5 feet by 9 feet and comes 90 percent preassembled. Prices vary, depending on leg design and ease of folding.

Wallace Leisure Products, Inc., 230 Fifth Avenue, Suite 1107, New York, New York 10001 **$60 to $100**

7. Removable feet permit this 27-by 51-inch screen to be used vertically, horizontally, or on the wall. The perforated hardboard panel is framed in northern maple. Would make a nice room divider, with artwork hanging on both sides.

Childcraft Education Corp.: 20 Kilmer Road, Edison, New Jersey 08817 **$30**

8. Handy orange polyvinyl playground bases can serve equally well as place mats, bath mats, or on bedside tables to catch spills from overturned glasses. They're light, washable, and adhere to clean floors.

Jayfro: P.O. Box 400, Waterford, Connecticut 06385
$21—three bases and home plate; $6—single base;
$7—home plate

9. Gleaming stainless-steel trays make excellent finger-painting accessories. Lay a few across the table, each filled with a different color, and let the kids be kids. Trays are seamless and clean easily. After the finger-painting stage, the trays can work as desk organizers, holding all those loose composition papers. Sizes range from 21¼ inches long and 16¼ wide down to 13⅝ by 9¾ inches.

Vollrath Co.: 1236 North 18 Street, Sheboygan, Wisconsin 53081 $10 to $30

10. Clay or play dough can get a tabletop pretty messy. So when the kids are sculpting, put down this polyethylene cutting slab and stop worrying. It's 18 by 24 by ¾ inches thick, and can be washed off in a jiffy.

Rubbermaid Commercial Products, Inc.: 3124 Valley Avenue, Winchester, Virginia 22601 $39

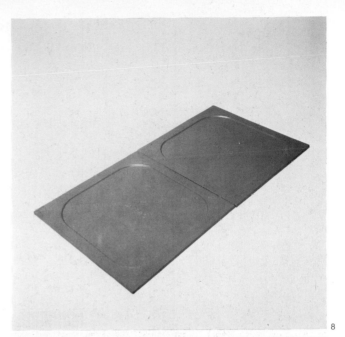

8

9

10

11. Children can hang all their
mementos on this black
magnetic board from Italy. Big,
bright metal-colored magnets
are optional, but would look
pretty against the black. Two
sizes: 18 by 27½ inches and 5½
by 18 inches.

Placewares: 13 Walden Street, Concord, Massachusetts
01742   **$13.95** and **$5.95**

12. Everyone loves the flexibility of
a bulletin board. Imagine how
much your child will enjoy one
filled with his or her homemade
cards, finger-painted creations,
and photographs.

Featuring a 2-inch oak frame
and natural tan cork, this one is
available up to 4 by 8 feet.
We're showing the 3- by 5-foot
size because it will work well
even in an apartment.

Claridge Products and Equipment, Inc.: PO. Box 910,
Harrison, Arkansas 72601   **$59**

11

12

13. An alternative to the traditional blackboard, this has a white porcelain enamel surface you write on with colored felt-tip markers. Creations are removed with a standard chalkboard eraser, and since chalk isn't involved, there's no dust or noise when the kids are scribbling. Measures 3 by 4 feet and comes with an aluminum frame, chalk tray, eraser, and one dozen assorted markers in red, blue, green, and black.

Claridge Products and Equipment, Inc.: P.O. Box 910, Harrison, Arkansas 72601 **$97**

14. Chalkboards have been hanging around schoolrooms for years— now it's time they hung out at home. One of the basic teaching aids, a chalkboard is the best place to show off the alphabet and multiplication tables. And learning can be a lot of fun if it's happening right in the child's bedroom. Once the kids have learned to read, the board is a great spot to leave messages.

This 3-foot-6-inch by 5-foot unit is small enough to hang at home. It features a chalk tray and satin anodized aluminum frame. The black Duracite surface reportedly outlasts ordinary painted boards. Also comes in green, which some educators say is easier on the eyes.

Claridge Products and Equipment, Inc.: P.O. Box 910, Harrison, Arkansas 72601 **$56**

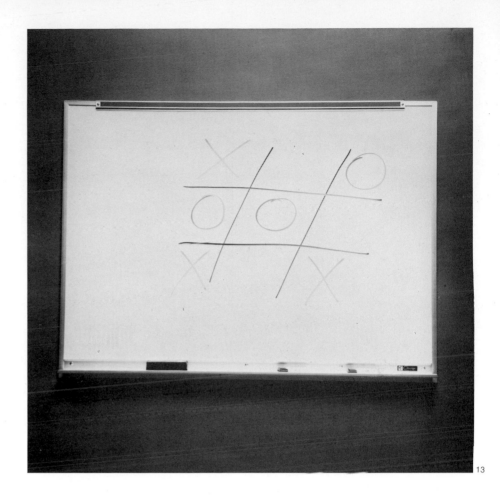

13

14

15

15. Kids can sit on big, plush pillows and gather around this nice low table to work, play, or have a party. Here a sturdy cast-iron restaurant base with black enamel finish supports the black laminate self-edge top. The table stands 13¾ inches high, and the 1¾-inch-thick top has a 30-inch diameter.

Although this base was custom-cut, standard 28¼-inch-high bases are available in varying dimensions, depending on the size and thickness of the table top used. Bottom spreads of the bases range from 18½ inches to 30 inches, with columns of 2 or 3 inches in diameter. Table tops range from 30 inches round or square to 60 inches, and are 1¼, 1¾, or 2 inches thick.

Bases come in a variety of finishes, including black crackle and black or colored porcelain enamel. Laminate tops are available in colors, patterns, and woodgrains. Choose your sizes, materials, and colors, and create your own table simply by attaching the top and base with screws.

We are indicating the price of the table shown here, but have not provided other sample prices because they vary greatly, depending on the type of top and base you pick.

L & B Products Corp.: 3232 Lurting Avenue, Bronx, New York 10469 $80—base; $55—top

16a

16. **Alvar Aalto** has three marvelous sturdy birch tables—two semicircles and one rectangle. Joined together, they form a 77¼-inch-long by 47¼-inch-wide by 23⅝-inch-high surface for big groups. The two semicircles together are 47¼ inches in diameter, and the rectangle is 47¼ inches wide by 30 inches long. You can also use each piece alone against a wall. All turns are rounded. Solid wood legs are sliced, bent, then glued into place. Tops are red or black linoleum or yellow, blue, red, or white plastic laminate.

International Contract Furnishings, Inc.: 145 East 57 Street, New York, New York 10022 $271—two semicircles with linoleum top; $291—with plastic top $144—rectangle with linoleum top; $150—with plastic top

16b

16c

17. Adjustable tables are ideal for kids since they provide different heights for different activities. This model measures 30 by 30 inches on the top and goes from 18 to 28 inches high in 2-inch increments. It's also available in other sizes. The base is nickel chrome-plated seamless steel tubing. The white surface is plastic laminate with oak edging.

Cameron-McIndoo U.S.A.: North Bennington, Vermont 05257   **$75**

18. Another adjustable table, this one stands on a four-legged black steel tube base and is used by professional photographers for posing products or babies. The height travels from 26 to 37 inches and a turn knob lets you swivel the top when the family is playing Scrabble. The blond melamine plastic surface measures 21 by 31 inches.

Ajusto Equipment Co.: 20163 Haskins Road, Bowling Green, Ohio 43402   **$66**

19. Your children want to invite friends over to do homework— but there isn't enough table space. That's the time it might be nice to have these cantilevered stacking worktables available. They make convenient snack areas, too. Frames are round steel tubing and tops are laminated, so they can be washed easily. Measures 24 inches wide by 20 inches deep by 29 inches high. The black bumper-edged top is offered in solids, woodgrains, and patterns.

Falcon Products, Inc.: 9387 Dielman Industrial Drive, St. Louis, Missouri 63132 **$72**

20. Tilt it up and it's a drawing stand; leave it flat and it's a desk. Appropriately called The Pupil, it can be adjusted to four different angles. The table is plastic-covered and the sleigh base is chromed or painted white, red, yellow, or green. Top is 23½ by 45¼ inches; stands 27½ inches high.

Inter/Graph, Ltd.: 979 Third Avenue, New York, New York 10022 **$240**

19

20

21a

21. Once your child has learned to use a typewriter, she'll probably be doing all her homework with it. A desk with detachable typing L lets the machine sit on one side, leaving the desk free for other work. The unit has a stain- and scratch-resistant plastic birch top and black enameled steel "modesty" panels. The pedestal is chrome with chrome-plated steel glides. If you're short of outlets, an optional electrical assembly is available built into the desk. Main desk is 20 by 42 by 29 inches high; machine platform is 18 by 24 by 27 inches.

Smith System: P.O. Box 3515, St. Paul, Minnesota 55165 $190

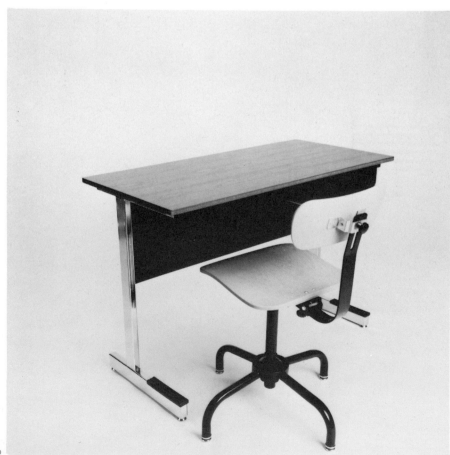

21b

22. A changing table is one of those necessities for baby, mom, and dad. This one is more than a changing table, and is actually billed as a writing desk by the manufacturer. The top raises, lowers, and tilts anywhere from 23¼ to 31½ inches, depending on where you place the pins in the base. It adjusts as your children grow and can stay with them from the diaper days until they've received their college diplomas. Styled in blond fir with a washable gray linoleum top measuring 59 by 27½ inches.

Scandinavian Design: 117 East 57 Street, New York, New York 10022 **$138**

23. The desk converts to an especially comfortable changing table when raised to maximum height and covered with a soft surface. We've topped it with a foam slab, which we covered in colorful Marimekko vinyl. The fabric can be wiped clean with a little soap and water.

Scandinavian Design: 117 East 57 Street, New York, New York 10022 **$138** plus cost of foam and fabric

22

23

24.

24. An alternative to the kitchen table for doing homework, this award-winning seating unit becomes an all-in-one study center. Optional writing arm and bookrack can be mounted without any tools. Seat and back are formed metal, finished with textured vinyl in a wide color range. For a warmer look, teak, walnut, and oak are also available. The seat is 17¾ inches high and 17¾ inches wide—contoured to hold big or little people. Schools and restaurants have been using this unit for years because of its utilitarian design, strength, and comfort. It fits in just as well at home.

G. F. Business Equipment, Inc.: East Dennick Avenue, Youngstown, Ohio 44501 **$90**

25. Another all-in-one homework environment has a full-front 19-by 24-inch desk top in brown or white patterned melamine, so overzealous writers can't mar it. The seat is a one-piece high-impact plastic shell in black, gold, blue, green, or bittersweet. High-strength square tubular steel forms the bright chrome-finished sled base. Steel-rod bookrack is optional on the biggest version and would certainly be a welcome addition. The seat is 17½ inches high, suitable for the high school or college set.

American Seating Co.: 901 Broadway N.W., Grand Rapids, Michigan 49504 **$62**

25.

26. Inexpensive but handsome and practical, this yellow plastic three-piece play set folds up and stores away in minutes. The 24-inch-square table stands 21 inches tall and has a textured nonmarring molded top. White-enameled steel legs fit into molded sockets and rest in a hidden leg rack when the table is collapsed. The folding chairs, also enameled steel, have contoured molded seats and locking mechanisms. This set is lightweight and therefore not ideal for toddlers, who often use chairs for support.

Cosco Home Products: 2525 State Street, Columbus, Indiana 47201 $33—set of table and two chairs; $10—each additional chair

27. When you don't have the space, but want to give your child a nice big work surface, consider a table that folds flat against the wall. Built on the cantilever principle, this 30- by 48-inch surface is fixed to the wall with a hinging system and swings out with the flip of a finger. The finish is melamine plastic, so even Magic Markers won't harm it. Comes in six colors, including butcher block, glazed oak, and white.

Sico, Inc.: 7525 Cahill Road, Minneapolis, Minnesota 55435 $153

26

27a

27b

28. This work or play surface is portable, big, and round so groups can sit together comfortably. It folds in half and can be pushed against the wall out of the way. The understructure and legs are square steel tubing, which provides good stability. The top is melamine plastic that comes in five finishes. It will serve equally well when the kids are doing homework or having a birthday celebration. Tops come 48 to 72 inches round.

Sico, Inc.: 7525 Cahill Road, Minneapolis, Minnesota 55435 **$146**—48 inches

29

29. Practically speaking, this table should get four stars. First of all, it has a polyurethane-laminated top, so water or soda pop won't seep in and deform it. The legs also disassemble easily for storage. Two heights are available: 19½ or 28 inches. Each top is 31 inches square. The short one could be used as a child's dining table and the tall unit as a work surface; or bring them outside for backyard barbecues. Big table comes in all white or black; little one only in white.

Beylerian, Ltd.: 305 East 63 Street, New York, New York 10022 **$220**—19½ inches; **$250**—28 inches

30

30. This quarter-circle table was designed for a school environment so the teacher could sit facing the children, but there's no reason why kids can't take turns occupying center stage. Measuring 48 inches overall and 20 inches high, the solid maple piece invites communication among playmates or workmates. Table top is ⅝-inch particle board laminated with maple-grain design plastic.

Community Playthings: Rifton, New York 12471 **$98.50**

31. Little stacking tables for little people's tea parties. Tops are red or white melamine set in a white rounded frame, on white enamel steel legs. Available in 20½- or 23-inch heights, each is 29½ inches square.

Krueger: 1330 Bellevue Street, Green Bay, Wisconsin 53408 **$48.50**—either height

31

32

32. Your young hobbyist will enjoy a high large work surface with bottom shelf. The top is 1¾ inches thick with hardwood core and high-density top and bottom surfaces. A retaining lip on the top and bottom shelves prevents tools from sliding off. H-frame square tube construction has adjustable rubber foot glides. Light tan, black, bamboo, or brown enamel. Also comes with optional three-outlet electrical assembly. Measures 24 inches deep by 60 inches long and 35 inches high.

Smith System: P.O. Box 3515, St. Paul, Minnesota 55165 **$270**

33. Young people always manage to have more notebooks, school supplies, and old compositions than they need. This desk lets them file it all away and still provides plenty of work space. It's a great play table, too. The three-drawer file cabinet base is topped by a 24- by 60-inch hunk of butcher block, so it only looks better as the child gets older. The drawers come in brown, white, or yellow, and can be labeled by very organized kids. Two-drawer file cabinets also available.

The Workbench: 470 Park Avenue South, New York, New York 10016 **$75** each—three-drawer file cabinet; **$70** each—two-drawer file cabinet; **$110**—top (butcher-block tops can also be purchased in many sizes at local lumberyards.)

34. A laminated maple or birch top sits on a metal locker base to form a combination work surface/storage area. The lockers are finished in gray baked-on enamel. Double swinging doors come with spring hinges and padlock attachment, or may be equipped with built-in locks. The locker opening is 36 inches wide, 21 inches deep, and 31 inches high with a center shelf. The overall unit is 60 inches wide, 28 inches deep, and 32¾ inches high. Other locker configurations are available, including double-face models for when there's more than one person working.

Lyon Metal Products, Inc.: P.O. Box 671, Aurora, Illinois 60507 **$230**

33

Sleeping

Before the invention of cribs, parents didn't worry too much where their babies slept. Often the infant would be hitched by a sling to the mother's hip, peacefully moving along with her and responding to the wonderful undulations of her body. At night, the baby would be placed in a makeshift sleeping arrangement on the floor.

Today, we have cradles, portable cribs, and regular cribs ... youth beds and big beds ... bunks, canopies, platforms, waterbeds, and trundles for when we get older. Where we put our children to sleep has become one of our primary considerations.

Babies can sleep anywhere. They really don't care whether it's in a crib, in a drawer, on the floor, or in a converted laundry basket. They just like warmth and confined space because they've recently come out of the womb. So you really don't have to run out and buy a crib right off. The cradle is the closest way to simulate the womb ... the walking, rocking motion of the mother.

1. Two young sisters sharing a 12-by 18-foot room doesn't make for the most ideal situation. So Bob Bray and Mike Schaible (Bray-Schaible Design) created a room on two levels with two identical environments.

The focal point: a wonderful carpeted bunk bed structure and a raised floor. One sister sleeps on the bottom level and gets to use half the room. The other sister climbs up the stairs on the right to reach the raised floor—and her bed. And when the sisters feel friendly, one can come to the other's level to play.

The raised portion of the room reaches up to the window, so the designers put two white enamel guardrails on the windows. The walls are shiny white and the industrial carpeting, which travels up the stairs and all over the beds, is dark charcoal. There's also a carpeted ledge to lean art on ... or just to sit against and think.

The mattresses are covered with charcoal-black chintz, then topped with lots of pillows in luscious colors like pink and yellow. That way they are more than beds and make comfortable, colorful sofas. "A child doesn't have to have a red (continued on page 89)

2. City kids really have it rough during the winters because they have no place to play outdoors. So Madelyn Ewing, a New York City mother, wanted to create an imaginative environment indoors for her New York City son, Douglas, and his friends. She got the idea for his room from the new playgrounds in New York that use fluid geometric structures to encourage children to use their bodies and, even better, their imaginations.

Almost everything in Douglas's room is built in and the space is broken up by lots of differ-ent platforms—for playing, working, sleeping, lazing. He climbs up the three-rung ladder to reach the upper level, which (continued on page 89)

(1. continued from page 84) wall," Bray says. The pillows provide the life.

There's storage room under the raised floor and bookshelves on the upper level. A typical air-conditioning unit is hidden under the floor and topped with a grille.

Like the room, the big plastic laminate worktable with pedestal base is divided in two, so each sister can do her homework without cramping the other. The divider can be removed when one wants a nice clear top on which to paint or sculpt. Rolling file cabinets in black are provided for each girl—to store notebooks, papers, and accessories. White Kevi chairs make sitting comfortable.

Luxo lights are mounted on the beds so when one wants to read the other can sleep. A track of dimmers can be turned all the way up for playing or down low for watching TV. The vertical window blinds are easy for kids to operate, Bray and Schaible say.

This is the kind of room that grows with the children. The raised levels are as much fun for kids playing cowboy as they are for young adults who want peace and quiet. And when one sister leaves home, the other can have both levels all to herself.

Bray-Schaible Design: 80 West 40 Street, Room 81, New York, New York 10018

(2. continued from page 87) stretches all across the room. The left part is his science lab and storage area; the right is a small, cozy space for reading. A spotlight can be clipped anywhere on the structure when Douglas wants to see what he's doing. The child is nine now and adores his dual-level room just as it is, but he can remove the cut-out structures later and use the top level as a gallery with bookshelves.

A series of raised platforms on the lower level have secret doors for kids playing hide-and-seek. And once they've outgrown that stage, there will be plenty of storage room. Two other platforms, covered with lovely blue Haitian cotton, act as beds or sofas. A sturdy red Kovacs light with a flexible neck sits between them.

The child's built-in desk is nice and big—8 feet long—and made of white Formica. Small spotlights with swivel bases are built into the platform above the work/play surface. Douglas also has his fish tank next to the desk—something he can look at when he gets tired of all those algebra calculations. He sits on a Kevi chair.

Gray industrial carpeting covers all the platforms. "I wanted kidproof carpeting," Madelyn says. The walls are all gray, with accents provided by the plush pillows. "The room is dark anyway since it overlooks a courtyard. Why try to make it look light when it can't be? Besides, kids can bounce balls against the wall and we don't see any marks."

"The room has worn well," she says—and that's the best testimonial a room can get.

The two narrow boys' rooms, on pages 88 and 89, share a common entrance and hallway with another similar-sized room. What designer Joe D'Urso wanted to do was create a sense of communication between the spaces yet maintain a feeling of privacy within each.

Although the rooms aren't exactly the same, a common feeling is evident through D'Urso's use of color and material. Both are painted white with warm-looking woods on the shelves and work surfaces, beautiful blues on the pillows and mattresses, hot orange-red on the storage systems. Cool black steel makes up the bunk bed in one room and the ladder in the other.

Since storage space is always a problem in small rooms, D'Urso put a wall full of Lyon's orange metal lockers topped with

butcher block in one and Republic Steel's orange basket rack in the other. Floor-to-ceiling open wood shelves hold books and small accessories, including Replogle's globe.

One boy sleeps on Folger Adams's black steel bunk bed and has a brass pole for sliding down when he wants to pretend he's a fireman. His brother climbs up a steel ladder to his built-in bed. A shelf under the sleeping arrangement is great for sitting, working, or storing.

Each child has an Inter/ Graph Pupil desk for doing homework and a Kevi chair so he'll sit right. Cork wall strips, one of D'Urso's favorite accessories, invite the boys to display their favorite posters. Track fixtures and Luxo lamps provide the lighting in both rooms. Windows are covered with white vertical blinds. Charcoal industrial carpeting by Wellco stands up to two boys or twenty and is easy to maintain.

And when one brother wants to take a peek at what the other is doing, he can look through their mutual porthole above the beds.

D'Urso Design: 80 West 40 Street, New York, New York 10018

Cradles take less space than cribs and are generally less expensive. Some people argue a cradle will only work for a short time—so why bother? It's really up to you. A carriage will work as well.

Once your child becomes aware of his surroundings and is too big for a cradle or portable unit, you'll probably want a crib. The best thing you can do is borrow one. Why spend anything when your friend or sister has a crib that's not being used?

Cribs come in a multitude of styles. Since the crib basically looks like a little prison, and doesn't get any design awards with Bo Peeps plastered on it, we've tried to select the cleanest models—for tastes ranging from traditional to contemporary. The ultimate is a solid, handsome chrome crib from Simmons. While more costly than most, it is a beautiful piece to look at and one of the safest around. It is the type of crib that can be passed on from generation to generation and look as new as it did from the start. Our selection is mainly limited to slatted cribs because they permit more ventilation and visibility than ones with closed sides.

Certain safety factors must be considered when buying a crib. The best buyer's source is *Consumer Reports*, which periodically updates what's on the market. Federal standards require that new cribs (1) have adequate rail heights, even when the drop side is lowered; (2) be fitted with strong locking devices for drop sides so children cannot release them; (3) be made in standard sizes so all mattresses and cribs will be suited for each other, thus avoiding dangerous gaps. Slats should be 2⅜ inches apart so the child cannot get his head between them. Hardware should be completely safe and attached so it cannot be removed by the child.

Although cribs are necessary confined areas from which there is no escape when a child cannot walk or climb, there are alternatives. Nancy Rambusch loves the floor. Ms. Rambusch, the head of New York City's Caedmon School, places her child on a mattress on the floor and surrounds it with big, hard-to-move carpeted platforms.

It's time to graduate from the crib stage when your child is walking and toilet trained. Then the sleeping possibilities are varied.

Not much can be said about conventional single beds except that they're places on which to sleep. Trundle beds save space and are good when two children share one small room.

Adult-size bunk beds are the most exciting because they're places to play and climb. They also provide great security. When the child is on the lower level, he's enclosed in a cozy environment. The top level can be turned into a loft play area by putting a piece of wood over it. Add loads of plush pillows to the top and a bookrack to make it into a private place for reading. A sheet draped over the bottom creates a closed environment; or, if you want to be more sophisticated, attach a pair of roller shades to the sides.

Some bunk beds have drawers underneath; others have shelf arrangements. Choose a bunk bed system with beds that separate, because your children may later prefer sleeping in separate rooms or next to one another. One European-designed arrangement not only separates but has beds that can be turned into good-looking sofas. Bunk beds should also have guardrails. Although a child shouldn't be sleeping on the top level until

4. You might have an easier time putting your young ones to sleep if they're getting into a bed that looks like a gigantic toy. Designed for playing, too, it has an optional two-step ladder —which, when turned on its side, also serves as a guardrail— and a big rolling drawer. White birch with brown, blue, yellow, or red sides. Overall dimensions are 80 inches long, 39½ inches wide, and 53 inches high. Comes knockdown and the beds can be separated.

Scandinavian Design: 117 East 57 Street, New York, New York 10022 $510—double-decker with two mattresses; $69—drawer; $29—guardrail/ladder (dealer) Muurame Lahtic, Finland (mfg.)

he's about five, it's best to have him protected even then.

Platforms, fairly easy to construct, are fun for children—and a change from the common box spring. Carpeting glued to the wooden platform will also hide carpentry imperfections. If you build a big enough platform, there can be room to play next to the mattress. A high resilient firm foam mattress works best.

Kids don't have to sleep on beds all the time; they might even be thrilled if you give them another option once in a while. Sleeping bags are snug, secure, and colorful and let kids pull in their environments. Some of the newest fillings make them as comfortable as mattresses. Children love sleeping bags for camping out right at home. They also come in handy for little overnight guests.

Cots are another alternative. They're inexpensive and easy to store. Or have you even considered hanging a hammock across a child's room? Ward Bennett, the designer, says he is "a hammock freak. They're comfortable, washable, and rock you to sleep." Although they're not recommended for overnight sleep, they're nice for naps or just playing. Besides, they're good for tired mothers and aching backs.

A portable bed is a lovely change from the traditional box spring and mattress. One mother attached four casters to a piece of plywood and covered it with a bright purple fabric. Then a mattress went on top, also covered with the beautiful material.

There's nothing like a good night's sleep. The way you decide to have your children bed down at night will make all the difference in the way they behave the next day.

5

6

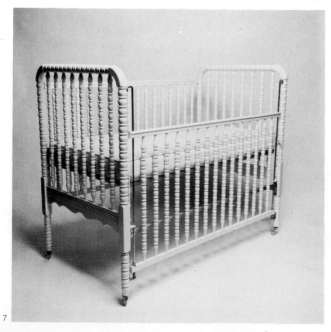

7

5. Clean lines, free of unnecessary Little Miss Muffet decals, distinguish this maple crib. It's full size—54 by 30 inches—with modern dowels on the ends and sides, and has steel stabilizer bars, plastic side teething rails, four-position spring, and heavy double drop sides. Rolls easily on four casters. Other cribs are available from this company, which is known for its clean design and natural wood finishes.

Childcraft: P.O. Box 444, Salem, Indiana 47167 $140

6. One crib that might be admired as much as the newborn infant. It's made of birch and coated with white lead-free plastic paint, with outside dimensions of 24¾ inches wide by 45¼ inches long by 35½ inches high. Adjustable to two levels for easy diaper changing. There's a black and white pocketed foam-padded vinyl fabric that wraps around the head and footboard (not shown). It will give baby something pretty to look at and you a place to stash a few toys. Comes knockdown. The side rails are stable, so it may be a chore to lift baby in and out.

Scandinavian Design: 117 East 57 Street, New York, New York 10022 $230—crib with mattress

7. One of the more popular styles for traditional nurseries, the Jenny Lind crib has been cradling babies for over thirty years. The look is available from many manufacturers. We're showing the model from Simmons's Juvenile Furniture line because of its solid reputation with mothers. It is styled in yellow, white, or maple finish or maple veneers and solids. There are plastic teething rails, nylon post brackets, and single or double drop sides. Length: 55 inches; width: 30⅛ inches; height: 46 inches. In the industry this company is particularly noted for its quality painted finishes.

Simmons Juvenile Products: 613 East Beacon Avenue, New London, Wisconsin 54961 $165

8. Not too many years ago, mothers put their babies to sleep in drawers when the family went traveling. Today, the portable crib lets baby sleep in comfort away from home. Although they're generally unsuitable for children over eighteen months, portable cribs are excellent when you're short of space. We think Port-a-Crib, the first portable crib, makes a handsome, respectable choice. Many apartment dwellers are even buying them instead of full-size models. It measures 27 inches by 42 inches, folds to a 6-inch width for easy storage, has adjustable legs so it can be converted to a playpen, and is the only unit that can be used in a dressing-table position. Most Port-a-Cribs also have casters, drop sides, and teething rails. They are the only portable cribs made of hardwood—maple, beech, or birch, with natural or walnut stain.

Graco Children's Products, Inc.: Elverson, Pennsylvania 19520 **$60**

9. Slightly larger than a portable unit, this wonderful white oak crib comes knockdown but is rigid enough to accommodate even the most restless babies. The vinyl-covered mattress, measuring 24 by 48 inches, can be positioned high or low for diaper changing or sleeping and takes standard-size contour sheets. The drop front features childproof fasteners. Designer Charles Webb says he dislikes large cribs because the baby gets lost in them. Besides, he adds, most children can be moved right from his crib into a bed. Overall dimensions are 26 by 50 by 42 inches high.

Charles Webb: 28 Church Street, Cambridge, Massachusetts 02138 **$200** (with mattress)

8

9

95

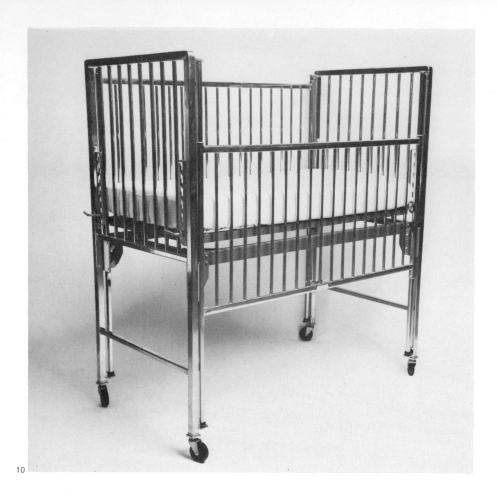

10.

10. Hospitals use this chrome-plated tubular steel crib. Although it's a big investment, it offers far more than conventional cribs. Measuring 36 by 54 inches, it will hold standard-size mattresses. The spring can be raised to between 32½ and 43¼ inches by lifting two handles at the head or foot and resting them in slots. These handles face away from the infant or child, making them impossible to dislodge. To lower or raise the side rails, you lift and press a trigger. There are three positions—two above the mattress and one below it so you can make the bed easily.

Bars are spaced so the child cannot get hurt. The top of the spring is 26 inches above the floor, and the crib rolls on 3-inch-high ball-bearing casters. You can also raise one part of the spring higher than the other should you want your baby's head to get some elevation. If you decide to make the investment, you can donate the crib to a hospital later on and take a tax deduction.

Thonet Industries, A Simmons Co.: 491 East Princess Street, York, Pennsylvania 17405 $660

11. What child doesn't like a bunk bed—not only for sleeping but for climbing and playing fort? Designed in white oak, this one has a sliding three-step ladder and three roomy drawers to hold clothes and toys. Endboards are paneled. Each bed measures 39 inches wide, so bedding down is comfortable at any age. The two levels are joined together with metal pins, but can be easily separated. Comes knockdown. A little clip-on table can be attached to either bed for nighttime needs.

Charles Webb: 28 Church Street, Cambridge, Massachusetts 02138 $325—bunk; $20—rail; $140—two mattresses; $35—clip-on table

11.

12. Two full-size twin beds can be used as bunks or unstacked when the kids are sleeping in separate bedrooms. Made of solid oak with a water- and scratch-resistant finish, these beds are joined by a decorative tongue-and-groove on one end and a drop-in wooden toe and cleat on the other. This makes it impossible for them to slide apart. The manufacturer says the unit is so sturdy that a 175-pound man can stand on the second rung of the lower bed and try to shake the upper bed without being able to budge it.

One side, with 4-inch-wide rungs, has been designed to be used as a ladder; the other end is a convenient 12-inch-wide five-shelf unit. A guard rail extends almost the entire length of the upper bunk. The mattresses, 39 inches by 75 inches each, are supported by a full size ¾-inch particle board, rather than the slat mechanisms commonly used in other bunk bed systems. Sixty inches high.

This system is expensive, but furniture experts praise its solid construction and high quality.

Tech Furniture: 917 Bridgeport Avenue, Shelton, Connecticut 06484 $765—two beds; $70—each mattress

13. Bright red, green, or yellow epoxy-lacquered tubing forms this marvelous bunk bed with its roomy optional schoolbag/pajama pocket. The natural canvas is edged with green on the red bed, red on the green bed, and blue on the yellow. The tube end caps are solid rubber to avoid scrapes when the kids are climbing all over. A swivel ladder and safety rail are included. Tubes are simple to dismantle so the bunks can convert into two single beds. The entire unit measures 78 by 66⅞ by 38½ inches. Mattresses covered in yellow, blue, or white cotton are optional.

Roche-Bobois U.S.A., Ltd. (New York and major cities): 200 Madison Avenue, New York, New York 10016 $495—bed with ladder and safety rail; $55—pajama pocket; $75—each mattress

12

13

14.

14. Crisp glazed cotton chintz pillows, beach balls, bed rolls, and bolsters provide glorious colorful splashes in a child's room. The pieces are wonderfully huggable—almost like sophisticated teddy bears—and, although they're somewhat costly, they'll be impressive accents in any room.

Each pillow measures 24 inches square and has a washable zippered cover. It comes in solids or multi-colored pieces of bold clear red, yellow, blue, purple, and green. The beach ball is 14 inches in diameter and comes in a striped nonzippered cover only. The striped bed roll, also washable, is 3 feet by 6½ feet and resembles a sleeping bag. The striped bolster is 8 inches in diameter and 3 feet long. It gives good back support when your youngster is reading in bed.

All pieces are stuffed with polyester fiberfill.

Girard Designs: 382 Lafayette Street, New York, New York 10003 $40—pillow (solid); $45—pillow (multi-colored); $50—beach ball; $100—bed roll; $45—bolster

15. Well-made equipment represents an investment that can be passed on from one child to the next. During those family backpack outings, it's important that children be kept warm and comfortable. The Little Foot sleeping bag is one of the best investments you can make. Children up to 5 feet 2 inches can sleep snugly in this 75-inch-long PolarGuard bag. (Camping experts believe continuous filament PolarGuard is the superior synthetic filling.) Mummy-shaped, it comes in blue or rust and has a roomy foot section and ample hood. There's enough air space and material for little people to be cozy and warm up quickly. Rolled, the bag is 7 inches by 18 inches, a size just right for kids to carry.

The North Face: 1234 Fifth Street, Berkeley, California 94710 $60

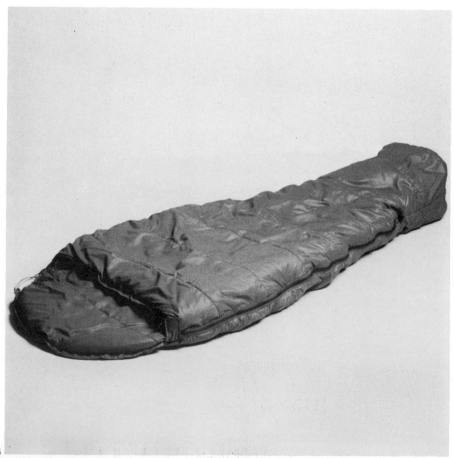

15.

16. Child-size sleeping bags are better than big ones for little people because they help children warm up quickly and efficiently. The Papoose, the 3-foot 6-inch sleeping bag at right, has been especially designed for infants and children up to the age of six. They should feel cozy resting here because the bag is filled with a man-made fiber, Hollofil, that feels almost as good as down. Although we don't expect you'll be taking an infant out in sub-zero weather, the Papoose has excellent insulating qualities. It would be an especially fine companion for a carriage. This baby bag comes in assorted color combinations.

Another sleeping bag in the same line is called Mogul Jr. and features the warmth efficiency of a mummy shape. It is styled to hold children aged six to fourteen. The outside is light blue and the inside gold, with Hollofil filling. The washable bag is 5 feet long and has a shoulder girth of 50 inches.

Pacific-Ascente: 1700 North Helm, Fresno, California 93727 $28—Papoose; $55—Mogul Jr.

16

17. And here's a roomy rectangular sleeping bag for older kids and grown-ups. Warm yet light-weight, it's available in two lengths, 6 feet or 6 feet 8 inches; each is insulated with six layers of polyester. Best of all, the Bare Bag has a zip-around foot that opens to make a fluffy cozy comforter. It can also go into the washing machine. Raspberry shell with dark blue liner.

Camp Trails Co.: 4111 West Clarendon Avenue, Phoenix, Arizona 85019 $65 and $69

17

18. Since kids can usually be found on the floor, why not give them a soft, comfortable place to sit or lay their bodies? This three-section pad is made of foam and covered with vinyl film. Measures 2 by 4 feet in 1-, 1½-, or 2-inch thicknesses. Comes in blue or green.

Tucker Duck and Rubber Co.: 2701 Kelley Highway, P.O. Box 4167, Fort Smith, Arkansas 72914 $8

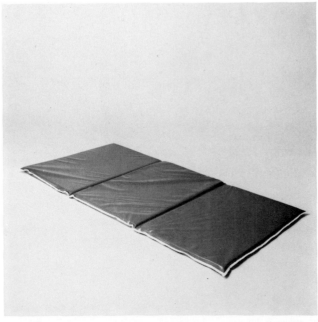

18

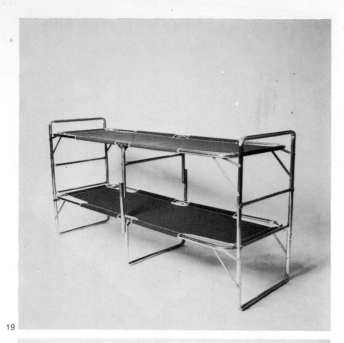

19.

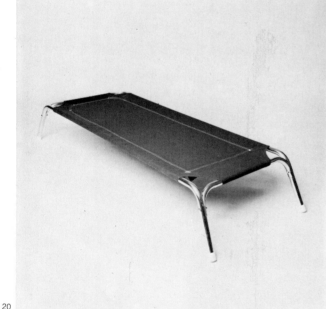

20

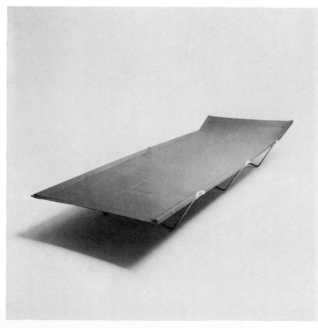

21

19. Double-decker folding cots provide extra sleeping space without taking up too much of the floor. This unit will fit well into many tents. The cots can be used separately as well. Polished aluminum furniture tubing is 1-inch extra gauge that supposedly won't rust, tarnish, or chip. All stress points are heavily braced and bar tacked. Green polyester canvas covers can be removed and replaced. Each cot measures 25 inches wide by 76 inches long.

Tucker Duck and Rubber Co.: 2701 Kelley Highway, P.O. Box 4167, Fort Smith, Arkansas 72914 **$35**

20. Nursery schools and kindergartens use stacking cots for nap time. Children can easily move them from room to room, or even outdoors for a rest in the fresh air. This lightweight model is made of heavy reinforced polished aluminum tubing with polyester canvas or woven plastic surface. It measures 22 by 53 inches, and comes in green or blue, with white rubber caps on the legs.

Tucker Duck and Rubber Co.: 2701 Kelley Highway, P.O. Box 4167, Fort Smith, Arkansas 72914 **$20**

21. If grandma doesn't have a bed to put up your five-year-old, send her over with a portable folding travel cot. That way she can spend the weekend getting spoiled. Three steel legs provide the resiliency of a spring bed. There are six side supports and a sturdy reinforced cover that assemble into a full-size cot.

Champion Industries: 35 East Poplar Street, Philadelphia, Pennsylvania 19123 **$20**

22. If you've got the space, imagine what fun everyone could have lolling in a hammock slung across the playroom. Kids might even line up to take their naps. This one is handwoven in cotton or polyester; both weaves are available in small, medium, or large sizes, from 10 to 14½ feet, with seasoned-oak stringers. Great in the backyard as well, between two trees or on an optional metal tri-beam stand.

This is the original rope hammock, fashioned in the 1880s by a riverboat pilot who grew tired of sleeping on grass-filled mattresses.

The Hammock Shop: P.O. Box 308, Pawleys Island, South Carolina 29585 **$46**—10 feet; **$66**—14½ feet

23. Champion race horses get treated pretty well. Sometimes they wear beautiful coolers in the most luscious colors. The company that manufactures these blankets will sell to anyone, even if you don't own a Seattle Slew. They're either 100 percent acrylic or a combination of wool and nylon, and measure 84 by 90 inches or 90 by 96 inches. They also can be stitched in contrasting colors with whipped edges. A bright red blanket with black stitching or a tan one with bright green would look smashing in a crib or on a bed. They're warm and soft, too. Several plaid patterns are available as well, from red and white to Victoria Scotch.

M. J. Knoud, Inc.: 716 Madison Avenue, New York, New York 10021 (dealer)
The Curvon Corp.: P.O. Box 865, Red Bank, New Jersey 17701 **$19**—84 inches by 90 inches; **$21**—90 inches by 96 inches (mfg.)

24. Van pads, those sturdy covers that protect your furniture while it's being moved from Los Angeles to Laredo, can go camping, to the beach, or stay at home on top of the bed. Made of 100 percent cotton, they come in only one size: 72 inches by 80 inches. A more expensive pad comes in brown and green or light and dark blue, and each is trimmed in red. A less expensive version is available in a random combination of the colors. The quality is the same with all pads; the only difference is the color consistency. All are stuffed with miscellaneous fibers, including polyester, nylon, and cotton.

Pads can be washed, although dry cleaning will add to their life. It also might be a sensible idea to spray on a protective coating, especially if the pads will be dragged around by the kids.

Acme Stayput Pad Co.: 295 Fifth Avenue, New York, New York 10016 **$17** (solid colors); **$10** (multi-colors).

25.

25. Canadian maple twin-size bunk beds come in four transparent colors (ruby red, sapphire blue, topaz yellow, and opal white) or clear maple. A urethane finish helps provide resistance to marring, abrasion, and spills when the kids are having cokes in bed. No matter which color you choose, the natural beauty of the grain is exposed. The clear maple, however, reportedly holds up better than the colored finishes; we also prefer it for its clean good looks.

The unit separates into two 3-foot 3-inch beds and is available with an optional two-drawer set on casters. A guard rail extends across the upper bunk.

A. Brandt: 1300 East Berry Street, P.O. Box 391, Fort Worth, Texas 76101 **$490**—two beds (white); **$506** (clear maple); **$527** (colors); **$363**—two mattresses and boxsprings; **$46**—ladder (white or clear); **$48** (colors); **$167**—two-drawer set on casters (white); **$170** (clear); **$177** (colors)

26. Young adults always love to have friends sleep over, and that's the time to slide out the trundle bed. A neat sleep setup for small bedrooms that just can't hold two beds, this duo is styled in white oak. The plain bed has a solid panel headboard and footboard. The trundle pulls out and raises to match the height of the top sleeper. You don't have to buy both beds at once; start with the top and add the bottom later on. Plain bed comes in widths from 30 to 54 inches and in queen and king sizes. Trundle is available 30 or 39 inches wide. An optional clip-on side table is a handy convenience.

Charles Webb: 28 Church Street, Cambridge, Massachusetts 02138 **$145**—39-inch plain bed; **$145**—39-inch trundle; **$70**—4-inch trundle mattress; **$35**—clip-on table

26.

27. **Milanese architect Vico Magistretti** designed this double-decker bed for his sons, but many adults separate top from bottom and use them as sofas with deep plush pillows. They look clear and fresh in solid beechwood, with natural, red, blue, brown, or green glossy aniline stain. Magistretti was one of the first designers to use aniline for furniture, claiming it lets the grain of the wood show through and gives it a certain thrill. If the aniline stain is too thrilling for you, choose white or black lacquer.

The bed requires a considerable amount of handcraftsmanship to produce and is a quality piece, suitable even for dormitory use. Each bed measures 81⅛ inches long, 34⅞ inches wide, and 29⅜ inches high. A set of three drawers, which mount to the bottom frame, is also available and is ideal for storing bedding and nightclothes.

Atelier International, Ltd.: 595 Madison Avenue, New York, New York 10022 $1340—double-decker bed with safety bar and ladder; $590—single bed; $180—each mattress, $590—set of drawers

27a

27b

28. Imaginative kids don't have to be outdoors to go camping or picnicking. They can do either right at home; and if they've got the right equipment, so much the better.

Help them set up an authentic camp site, and they'll probably play for hours. Sunshine Cover and Tarp's 6-foot diameter tent (which goes up in just 10 seconds) will hold a few youngsters comfortably and act as a great protector from the "outside" world. The child-size Mogul Jr. sleeping bag is from Pacific Ascente, and the bright red horse cooler from Curvon Corp.

Palco's canteen and stainless steel cup will serve well when the kids start yelling for drinks and snacks.

And the Camp Trails' Mee Too backpack can hold toothbrushes, pajamas, and slippers ... when the children get ready to bed down for real.

Sunshine Cover and Tarp, Inc.: 20310 Plummer Street, Chatsworth, California 91311 $75

29. Barrett Foa has something special in his room—a stage. The gently curving platform dominates the room, and although it holds a Simmons chrome crib now, it can just as easily take on a mattress. Eventually, a blue curtain will hang from a chrome rod and follow the lines of the platform. What fun Barrett and his friends will have drawing the curtain shut and hiding behind it. Or maybe he'll write a play and stage it in his bedroom. When Barrett gets older, he can close the curtain and create a private space.

Right now the 31-inch-high Lyon metal cupboards below the window hold all the accessories of infanthood, but they will surely hold Barrett's bats, balls, and Little League T-shirts in a few years. The top is white Formica edged in aluminum, providing a nice big work surface.

As he did with brother Justin's room, designer Joe D'Urso carpeted part of this one in charcoal gray and did the front third in black vinyl tile. D'Urso also ran carpeting partway up the wall "since it's a warm surface for a crawling infant." A cork map rail meets the top of the carpeting so Barrett can display art or his "A" compositions.

A semi-enclosed platform at the rear of the room is fitted with a laminate butcher block surface. Now it is used as a changing area, but will become the child's work center in a few years. "Barrett can sit at the desk doing homework and look out the window," D'Urso says. Lyon's gray rolling tool chest nestles below the platform. Mack Molding's plastic cubes hold towels, diapers, and blankets for now, and the maid's baskets by Harloff make cotton, ointments, and creams readily available. More shelves will eventually go near the desk, and so will a red Kevi chair.

Vermont Tubbs's snowshoe adult rocker and child's canoe chair provide additional seating. The rocker is especially convenient for nursing. Inter/Graph's BoBy sits next to the crib.

D'Urso Design: 80 West 40 Street, New York, New York 10018

Eating

The items on the following pages help you prepare, serve, and store food and drink when there's a child among the diners. A number of them are aimed directly at those parents who prefer fresh food to processed, who want to make baby food from scratch so they know exactly what's going into it.

Manual baby-food grinders have been around for years, but have never been as popular as they are today. They're easy to use, easy to wash, and grind out just the right amount of food. Besides, preparing your own baby food is certainly less expensive than buying it—and usually healthier. Some big companies are even manufacturing electric grinders and mini food processors. Though they are more costly than manual devices, they offer a number of attachments for preparing different food consistencies. Food mills provide another way to make grown-up food into baby food. They're also wonderful for older people who must have their food puréed.

1. Often young children imitate their parents. It makes them feel grown-up and important. Kids especially like to cook. If you want to thrill your youngsters, set up a miniature kitchen and give them a place where they can use their pots and pans.

Community Playthings makes stove and sink units that look almost real. They're made of solid maple and measure 24 inches high by 24 inches wide by 13 inches deep.

Other kitchen accessories here include Anchor Hocking's cookie jars and Vollrath's stainless steel trays.

Community Playthings: Rifton, New York 12471
$59.50—stove and sink combination

Of course, there's more to life than puréed bananas, mashed carrots, and ground meat. Machines that make ice cream, yogurt, or popcorn are great when groups of kids get together and make their own treats. And no one says you can't whip up a quart or two of ice cream when the children aren't home.

Other items are designed to make life around the kitchen a little easier. New mothers are constantly heating up small portions, so small pots and skillets will come in handy. A set or two of storage containers will be welcome when you want to save leftovers. Ice cube trays are perfect for freezing a week's worth of meals. Each cube is just about the right size for an infant's portion. Simply drop a frozen cube into a small pot and heat it up.

A hot pot, double boiler, and pressure cooker are also good staple kitchen equipment. "The electric hot pot is especially nice in a no-kitchen situation when you want to heat water for soup or spaghetti," says Mimi Sheraton, *New York Times* food critic. A double boiler keeps food warm for long stretches when one child is eating at 6:00 and another at 7:30. Pressure cookers are great for making vitamin-packed fresh steamed vegetables quickly and economically.

Then there are the items that can make life around the table more pleasant. Children love colorful dinnerware and items with handles for grabbing. Plates, cups, and glasses kids can call their own might make them enjoy eating more.

Plastic utensils, which come in lots of bold bright colors, are best for youngsters who don't

know that things break when they drop. Older children can graduate to breakable eating utensils. Special items make eating entertaining; one five-year-old uses his charming Wedgwood set every day because he loves the Peter Rabbit pictures that run around the plate and mug.

"A child can also learn good taste and manners from the way a table is set," says Elaine Cohen, president of the furniture firm DIA. "If parents are messy when they're eating, kids will be too," she adds. Pretty table accessories, such as fresh flowers or place mats, will teach children that breakfast, lunch, and dinner are times to savor. See-through place mats let children be creative because photographs, drawings, or prints can be placed in them and changed daily.

Silver cups are also appealing to children; they're cool, fun to touch, and might possibly become heirlooms. Almost everyone has a childhood cup that brings back lovely memories. Stainless-steel cups are ideal bedside companions for children who get up in the middle of the night and want water or juice. They don't break or chip, and—like silver—are extremely sanitary and pleasantly cool when they hit the lips.

Outdoor eating accessories—canteens or all-in-one fork, spoon, knife combinations—will be convenient when you're in the park and want to serve juice rather than soda, yogurt rather than hot dogs. It's often been said that we are what we eat. How we eat counts, too.

2. Special friends or relatives will light up when you give them a sterling silver porringer or baby cup. The porringer has a 4½-inch diameter and the cup stands 2½ inches high. Both are available in all silver or with pink or blue glaze linings. They make elegant, practical baby gifts. Reed & Barton: 144 West Britannia Street, Taunton, Massachusetts 02780 $65—porringer; $45—cup

3. A 1-quart large-mouth insulated canteen carries fresh juice for screaming youngsters who want a drink at the strangest times. High-impact green plastic with polystyrene insulation, both for hot or cold liquids. The polypropylene strap is adjustable or removable.

Serve the juice in a stainless-steel drinking cup that will fit into a back pack or handbag. It has a rolled edge with stay-cool lip and wire handle. Palco Products: P.O. Box 88, Slatersville, Rhode Island 02876 $8.00—canteen; $2.50—cup

4. Your child's name can be engraved up the side of this sterling silver beaker. It'll be great for juice at first, and mint julep much later on. Choose printed or script letters. This is one cup that will be used by your child through adulthood. Reed & Barton: 144 West Britannia Street, Taunton, Massachusetts 02780 $75—plus engraving

5. Sometimes you want to feed your children wholesome snacks outdoors but would prefer not to carry four different utensils. So do what the campers do: carry a combo knife. This one has a high-carbon cutlery steel blade, stainless-steel fork and knife, and bottle-top opener. It'll let you feed them yogurt or tuna in the park instead of potato chips. Palco Products: P.O. Box 88, Slatersville, Rhode Island 02876 $5

2

4

3

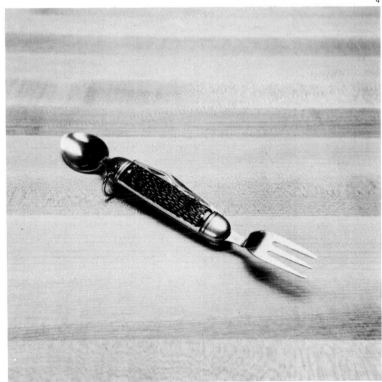

5

6

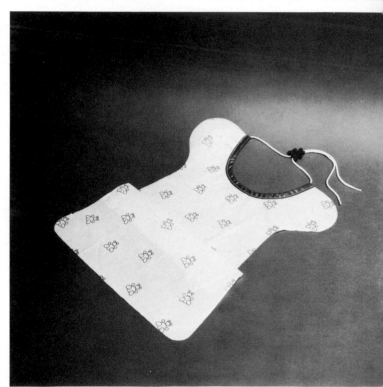

114

6. People today prefer preservative-free food for themselves and, of course, for their babies. One way to ensure that your infant gets the freshest foods possible is by preparing them yourself.

The Nurtury is the ultimate infant feeding system for making home-cooked foods for babies up to two years old. The backbone of the system is a motor-driven grinder that works on any cooked food, including meat. Three steel texturizing disks are provided for a choice of consistencies: purée, junior, or toddler. The food goes into the tube, is plunged through the disk, and drops into a serving dish. The grinder works masterfully, is easy to use, and is a snap to clean. It comes packed with three 4-ounce dishwasher-safe storable servers.

Other complementary items are available individually or in sets. One set includes a baby-food warmer that warms up to three portions in ten to fifteen minutes. A serving tray stores on top of the textured-glass surface of the warmer. The tray holds three storage cups and features a suction cup, which allows it to sit firmly on a high chair tray or table.

Another set of accessories has a 3-ounce drinking tumbler with a lock-on lid that controls liquid flow. It's made of high-impact unbreakable plastic. There's also a stainless-steel feeding spoon for mother that holds food close to the tip for easy feeding, and a baby's perforated self-feeding spoon. A plastic-coated nylon bib has a large pull-open pocket to catch spills. The bib is soft and lightweight and doesn't get in baby's way. It can be laundered in an automatic washer and dryer and is one of the best bibs around.

Teledyne Water Pik: 1730 East Prospect Street, Fort Collins, Colorado 80521 $95.00—all pieces; $45.00—grinder, three storage containers; $35.00—warmer, tray, three storage containers; $14.00—tumbler, two spoons, bib, three storage containers; $3.95—tumbler; $4.95—bib; $4.95—package of six storage servers; $2.95—baby's or mother's spoon

7

8

9

7. Food mills strain, mash, rice, and purée everything from cooked carrots to apples. They even make pâtés and turn jams into sauces. Food mills are handy for mothers, who must strain baby's first vegetables and fruits. Made of high-grade stainless steel, this model is efficient and easy to operate, with removable parts that facilitate thorough washing. We love to use it for making batches of applesauce for baby and family. It comes with three disks: all-purpose; superfine, for making baby food; and coarse, for green beans, strawberries, or nuts. You can fit the three adjustable feet on the base over the rim of a bowl and grind directly into it.

Mouli Manufacturing Corp.: 1 Montgomery Street, Belleville, New Jersey 07109 $8

8. Lightweight plastic flasks are ideal containers for taking juice to the park or dispensing shampoo in the bath. Flat and compact, they'll fit into Mom's handbag or Dad's hip pocket. They're also airtight, so you'll never have to worry about spills. Made in Finland, they hold 10 ounces of liquid and come in a variety of colors.

Wings Over the World Corp.: 225 Fifth Avenue, New York, New York 10011 $2 each

9. When you're in a no-kitchen situation with the kids and want to heat a bottle, make some cocoa, or even prepare spaghetti, boil water quickly with this Hot Pot. Made of seamless aluminum with a bright red acrylic exterior, the pot features a safety lock-on lid, black phenolic handles, and a heatproof base. The 600-watt unit has a detachable cord and stands 8 inches high. Would also be great for college dorm rooms.

West Bend Co.: P. O. Box 278, West Bend, Wisconsin 53095 $24

10

11

12

13

By the time your kids grow up, the metric system will be a way of life. You might try teaching them metrics now. A clear plastic 6½-inch-high pitcher, with milliliter and liter markings, can make the learning exercise fun. The handle has been designed for young children, and the lip shape almost guarantees controlled pouring.

Didax, Inc.: P.O. Box 2258, Peabody, Massachusetts 01960 $6.50

A little Julia Child or James Beard at home can imitate mommy or daddy with this realistically styled cooking combo. All-aluminum, the set comes with 5- and 6-inch saucepans, 7-inch frying pan, 5½-inch complete coffee percolator, four graduated measuring cups, and measuring spoons. Every piece can be used for real-life cooking, too.

Community Playthings. Rifton, New York 12471 $12.50 —the set

Seven aluminum English-made pitchers starting with 10 little milliliters all the way up to 2 liters are designed to illustrate volume to schoolchildren. They'll be handy around the kitchen and another way for you and your family to learn the metric system. Different-colored handles help young people to distinguish one liter from a half and a quarter. Each pitcher has two lips, to accommodate both right- and left-handed children.

Didax, Inc.: P.O. Box 2258, Peabody, Massachusetts 01960 $65—the set

The second petite chef at home can work with another cooking set—lidded teapot, deep covered kettle, ladle, saucepan, and frying pan. It's made of heavy-gauge aluminum, and you'll find the kettle and saucepan ideal for heating baby's bottle or small portions of food.

Creative Playthings: Princeton, New Jersey 08540 $16 —the set

When you want to prepare only one lamb chop or heat up a

14

15

16

little bit of soup, think about using a small saucepan or skillet. Cast-iron ware is recognized by the pros because it conducts heat evenly and gradually. The two pieces here, by Le Creuset, are coated with tan vitreous enamel that's highly heat-resistant and keeps tiny food particles from sticking. It's good for roasting, simmering, or cooking over low heat. Some pieces also come with a dull black enamel lining for frying over high heat. The 26-ounce saucepan has a wood handle, and the 6-inch skillet comes with an iron handle. Both pieces are available with brown, flame red, or yellow exteriors.

Schiller & Asmus, Inc.: 1525 Merchandise Mart, Chicago, Illinois 60654 $22—saucepan; $10—skillet

15. Your children may learn to love vegetables if they're prepared in a pressure cooker. All the vitamins stay in—and so do the color and flavor. Pressure cooking is also very fast. Appropriately, one of the best cookers comes from a company named Presto. If you're concerned about safety, this model features an air vent/ locking system that allows pressure to build only when the cover is closed correctly. The cover cannot be removed until the pressure is safely reduced. Other features include a pressure regulator, a heatproof handle, and a flat bottom. The 4-quart unit here is stainless steel, although polished aluminum is also available.

National Presto Industries, Inc.: Highway 53 North, Eau Claire, Wisconsin 54701 $42

16. A 2-quart heavy-duty stainless-steel saucepan and double boiler will not only come in handy at bottle-heating time, but will also help make cereals smooth and creamy. Straight handles are welded to the pans and have holes for hanging. The 2-quart double boiler inset has a rounded bottom for stirring. Bases are aluminum for good heat distribution.

Vollrath Co.: 1236 North 18 Street, Sheboygan, Wisconsin 53081 $43—covered double boiler; $15—saucepan

17.

17. Giant 14-ounce plastic Rainbow mugs for big drinkers live up to their name: a set of six includes one each in hot pink, kelly green, purple, lemon yellow, navy, and orange. They work with hot or cold beverages and are stackable. Seven-inch plates come in matching hues. The whole rainbow would look pretty at a birthday party table, with each guest choosing his or her favorite color. Also available in sets of one color.

Heller Designs, Inc.: 460 Ogden Avenue, Mamaroneck, New York 10543 $10.00—six-mug set; $2.50—each plate

18. What child wouldn't eat his spinach if he knew he'd see Mr. McGregor chasing Peter Rabbit when the plate was clean? Wedgwood's china bowl, plate, and mug set is a mealtime favorite, telling the story of Peter Rabbit in words and charming drawings by Beatrix Potter. The bowl is practical— wide and shallow, so hot foods cool quickly. A two-egg coddler can be purchased separately (as can each piece in the set); it's great for heating up small amounts of food.

Wedgwood: 41 Madison Avenue, New York, New York 10010 $25.00—the set; $9.00—bowl; $7.50—plate; $8.50—mug; $12.00—egg coddler

18.

19. Babies need sensible eating utensils, and Tommy Tippee makes a respected line that's sensibly priced, too. Its well-known Roll-y Poll-y cup has a weighted base to reduce spilling and two training lids to help the child progress to cup drinking. The cup is molded in heat- and shatter-resistant plastic. The polypropylene juice cup also comes with a spout lid. Both are 4 ounces. Available in pastels and white.

Westland Plastics: 800 North Mitchell, Newbury Park, California 91320 $2.00—Roll-y Poll-y; $.60—juice cup

19

20. It's 3:00 A.M. and your five-year-old decides he wants a drink of water. A stainless-steel tumbler will last through lots of after-midnight thirsts and never break. Tumblers hold 7 or 12 ounces; drinking cup with handle is 9 ounces. Stainless steel may be more expensive than plastic, but its sanitary properties make it popular, especially in hospitals. Consider using it for your children, especially in the bathroom.

Vollrath Co.: 1236 North 10th Street, Sheboygan, Wisconsin 53081 $3 and $4—tumblers; $7—drinking cup

20

21. Those little bits of leftovers sometimes make great after-school snacks or, with a little ingenuity, new meals. One place to store anything that's left on the dinner plate is in these plastic food savers. They can also be popped into the freezer, a big help when you want to be prepared for next week's meals.

The white, red, yellow, brown, biscuit, or green tops have two layers for a snug fit. The clear dishwasher-safe containers come in sizes and shapes to fit all kinds of foods. We're showing the 5-ounce size here because it's ideal for miniature portions.

Copco, Inc.: 11 East 26 Street, New York, New York 10010 $2—5 ounces

21

22. If you don't think you need the fancy electric grinder, there are manually operated models that perform just as well, although as yet they don't have different disks for different textures. Happy Baby Food Grinder is the original, designed by a doctor who thought there must be a better way to feed babies than with commercially prepared foods. Made of polypropylene plastic with a stainless-steel disk, it grinds the same meat, fruit, and vegetables you eat, in portions small enough for infants. After you've ground the food, the disk and handle come out so baby can be fed right from the base.

Available in three models; the largest comes packed in a little plastic lunch pail so you can take it to Grandpa's. Can be sterilized or washed in the dishwasher. Deluxe grinders hold 4½ ounces; economy model holds 4 ounces.

Bowland-Jacobs International, Inc.: Fox Industrial Park, Yorkville, Illinois 60560 $8.50—deluxe grinder, Tote Along, spoon; $7.50—deluxe grinder and spoon; $6.00—economy grinder

23. You don't absolutely need this, but it will certainly put smiles on everyone's face: an ice cream maker that prepares two flavors at once and is easy enough for a five-year-old to work. There are two 1-quart containers. Fill one with ice cream ingredients and the other with yogurt. Surround them with regular household salt and ice. Twenty-five minutes later you can have a sundae party.

Norelco, Consumer Products Division: 100 East 42 Street, New York, New York 10017 $45

24. If you start early, your children may learn to love yogurt as much as ice cream. One way to help cultivate their taste is to make natural fresh yogurt at home—from scratch. It's more delicious than what you can buy in the store, and less costly. This electric yogurt maker has five serving jars and is easy to use; all you need is milk and starter. A recipe book, included, explains what to do when you want more exciting flavors than vanilla.

Salton, Inc.: 1260 Zerega Avenue, Bronx, New York 10462 $13

25. Unlike the Nurtury, which only grinds, La Petite Machine chops, purées, and blends like a mini food processor, and can process meat into pieces small enough for an infant to digest. The package includes a cutting/chopping unit; double-bladed, stainless-steel cutting knife; tool for removal and replacement of the knife; and a Blendizer attachment. The housing, blender, and chopping unit are plastic. The machine is good-looking, so it can be brought right to the table and food served directly from it. Dimensions are: 8⅜ inches high, 10⅜ inches wide, and 5⅝ inches deep. The motor is ⅗ horsepower. The same company also makes a grown-up version called La Machine.

Moulinex Products, Inc.: 400 Conner Center West, Pennsauken, New Jersey 08109 $50

24

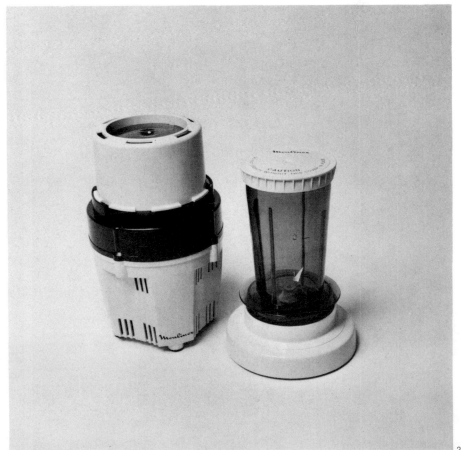

25

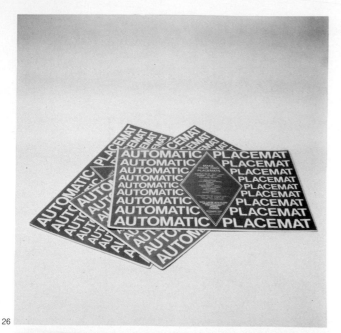

26

26. Members of the fidgety set may sit at the table longer if their place mats show a favorite drawing, cartoon, or photograph. Styled in washable see-through plastic, the Automatic Place Mat opens like an envelope, so material can be changed daily or for each meal.

Wings Over the World Corp.: 225 Fifth Avenue, New York, New York 10010 $2.50—each

27

27. Narrow, flexible, and rustproof, this is one of the best-designed baby-bottle brushes around. It has a wood handle and resilient white nylon bristles. The center is plastic-coated wire that can bend in any direction, reaching into small bottle corners to scrape out those dried layers of formula or fruit juice. Measures 17¼ inches long.

Lola Products Corp.: 100 Louis Street, South Hackensack, New Jersey 07606 $1

28. Cleverly designed so that the spoon and fork slide neatly into the knife handle, this three-piece stainless steel set will make a nice outdoor companion. Stash it in your handbag and take the trio to the park so you can give the kiddies apple slices or cheese when they get ravenous. Great also for campers and picnickers. The knife is serrated.

Marks International, Inc.: 60 Wells Avenue, Newton, Massachusetts 02159 $6

28a

28b

29. No kitchen is really complete without a cookie jar. And if you don't want to fill it with cookies, how about using it to store flour, sugar—even cotton balls in the nursery? These jars look kind of old-fashioned and are used today by stores to hold penny candy and dried fruits. They're styled from machine-made glass and have shiny polished metal lids with pretty red knobs. They sit on their sides so the openings face front, making it easy to get to what's inside. One- and two-gallon sizes are available.

Anchor Hocking Corp.: Pierce and Fifth Avenues, Lancaster, Ohio 43130 $5—1 gallon; $7—2 gallons

29

30. Corning's 15-ounce bowl has a smooth, curvy handle kids can grab on to, so the company has called it Grab It. Beautifully plain in white, it travels from freezer to oven to table, works in microwave ovens, and can be used on top of the stove to reheat leftovers. Good for morning cereal or after-school ice cream sundaes.

Corning Glass Works, Consumer Products Division Corning, New York 14830 $8- two-bowl set

30

31. These round stainless-steel bowls have tight-fitting plastic covers, to protect what's inside. Instead of preparing lots of little portions, make a large amount and save some till the next meal. The bowls are great to carry along on picnics or to the beach. Use them to mix, warm, and serve as well.

Sizes start at 12 ounces and go to 4 quarts. The 12-ounce bowls shown here are perfect for holding portions for several baby-size meals and will last long after your offspring has left home. The plastic lids may be replaced with tops from standard nut or coffee cans.

Vollrath Co.: 1236 North 18 Street, Sheboygan, Wisconsin 53081 $2 to $6

31

32. Justin's Foa's room has been designed for the utmost in practicality. The floor has been divided so that two-thirds is carpeted and the remainder is maple hardwood covered with polyurethane for durability. That way, when Justin wants to paint or use water, he can sit on the uncarpeted portion and his mother doesn't have to be concerned about spills.

A 26-inch-high permanently installed work surface spans both the hardwood and carpeted sections and is canti-levered so it looks like it's floating in midair. Lyon's locker room bench sits on one side and Ajusto's stool on the other.

A whole wall of open wood cubbies below the window holds Justin's possessions. He's got them very well organized, with similar items together in each cubby. That way he knows just where to look for a ball or a boat. As soon as friends visit Justin's room, they make a beeline for the bed. But this is no ordinary sleeping arrange-ment: it's a two-level wood and steel structure that designer D'Urso likes to think of as a "room within a room."

"The height of the ceiling lets me create a big top level for playing. Kids can sit on this cozy carpeted platform and look out at the rest of the room," D'Urso explains. A guardrail protects kids who get too excited. Children love to survey what's happening below them and enjoy a territory that's off limits to adults. When Justin becomes an adult himself, he'll probably want to use the top as a reading nook. For now, he can take his sleeping bag to the top when he feels like "camping out." The mattress on the lower level rests on a carpeted platform that also has plenty of play space.

Storage space doesn't stop there. Justin has totes and trays to hold small things; Shure's big red rolling tool chest for bigger things; United Metal's shiny chrome dome for laundry; and its red, white, and blue basket for bats, skis, and other tall items. Bisley's file cabinet by the bed doubles as a night table, with a Luxo lamp ready to light up. A Community Playthings block cart helps organize even further.

There's a tall Luxo on a T-stand by the desk, but it can easily be moved to any other part of the room. Designer Joe D'Urso also ran a cork display rail along one wall to show off the child's budding talents. The window is covered with vertical blinds, easy for the boy to adjust.

This is the kind of room that lets a child play and work without too many restrictions. Chances are Justin will adore it, even when he and his future wife visit for a weekend years from now.

D'Urso Design: 80 West 40 Street, New York, New York 10018

Seating

There are different seats for different people. Swivel chairs for secretaries. Canvas chairs for directors. Dentist's chairs for uneasy patients. Big overstuffed chairs for fathers who watch football games. Plush leather ones for bosses. Rockers for grandmas. And grown-ups aren't the only people who need special seats—little kids do, too. During your child's first seven years, you'll need at least eight chairs. The three staples for the earliest years are a high chair for eating, a booster seat for reaching the table, and an infant seat for watching mom.

No matter which models you choose, the first and major consideration should be safety. Since this is such a substantial topic on its own, we've read through consumer guides, talked with some experts, and come up with a choice selection for each type of chair. Cosco copped the top honors with its high chair, booster, and infant seats. Other brands are available that may or may not be as safe.

When choosing a high chair, look for a safety restraining system, a positive-lock tray, legs with

a wide stance, and rounded rather than sharp edges. A chair should never fold under the baby's weight. A booster seat should stay put so the tot won't slide around and fall off, and it should draw close to the table. An infant seat should have a safety strap, a seat adjustment device that locks securely, and a nonslip surface, and should be free of sharp edges or parts. The base should be wider than the seat to provide maximum security.

Right after your child graduates from the highchair-booster-seat stage, she'll probably be spending a lot of time sitting on the floor. "Children are floor people," says designer Ward Bennett. "It's less confining than a chair. Kids' muscles are loose and limber, and they prefer moving around in a big territory." It's when they're off the floor that you've got to start thinking about what additional chairs will make them —and you—happy. You won't want to buy fifteen different chairs for fifteen different purposes;

1. How easy it will be to get them to sit down if there's a chair with their name right on the back. Modeled after the grown-up version, the children's director's chair has a white-finish hardwood frame which comes knockdown. Seat and back are vinyl-coated polyester in blue, red-orange, lime, or yellow. Letters iron on and are included. Seat height: 12½ inches; width: 16½ inches; depth: 13½ inches; overall height: 23½ inches.

   Gold Medal, Inc.: 1700 Packard Avenue, Racine, Wisconsin 53403 $23

2. Sit with your children in matching director's chairs. This youth version measures 19¼ inches wide by 28¼ inches high with a 15-inch seat height, and can hold older and bigger youngsters than the one from Gold Medal. The natural hardwood frame is varnished and supported by metal braces. Water-repellent slip-on seat and back are 18-ounce heavyweight custom-dyed canvas.

   The adult model is 24 inches wide by 33 inches high with a 17-inch seat height. The little model is available in red, yellow, blue, green, or orange; grown-ups get a choice of thirteen additional colors, including beige, black, white, and brown.

   The Telescope Folding Furniture Co., Inc.: Church Street, Granville, New York 12832 $30 and $38

space alone will preclude that. So make sure the chairs you choose work for several purposes and make sense for more than a year or two. And keep safety in mind; children will climb on anything. Any chair you choose should be sturdy or else it could tip, even under the weight of a one-year-old.

There are five basic activities that require a different seat: eating, relaxing, reaching, group play, and intensive work such as writing. A wide variety of chairs is available to suit each need. Before you choose any, consider what children like. Kids like chairs that move—rockers, chairs on wheels, soft plushy chairs. That way they have more control over them and can drag them wherever they go. They especially like chairs that conform to their little bodies, chairs that take them around and make them feel secure.

A beanbag and child-size rocker are probably two of the smartest purchases you can make. "Even little kids get tense watching *Mr. Rogers*," says Stan Berenstain, author of the Berenstain bear books. "A rocker is responsive. You sit in it, push, and it goes. You can make it stop when you want," adds Robin Berenstain, Stan's daughter-in-law and head of a Denver day-care center. Rockers can calm a crying child, too, and they're wonderful for your youngster to sit in and watch you nurse the baby. A beanbag is the next best thing to a mother's hug, Robin also thinks. "When mom's not around, a kid can plop in a beanbag and let it comfort him. That's why children love big, fat, ugly, overstuffed chairs," Robin says. When you buy a beanbag, however, make sure the filling is fire-retardant.

Children relate better at first to chairs that are close to the floor. "Their feet don't reach the ground when they're on regular-size chairs, and it starts to annoy them if it happens all the time," says Marion Pasnik of the New York City Board of Education. "Low foam seats are great for reading. They're comfortable and child-size."

When kids are old enough to get together in groups and sit still, they like molded plastic chairs because they're smooth and somehow soothing. Lots of plastic chairs stack, so you can buy a few and put them away easily when group play is over. They also come in bright colors, take to being scribbled on, and are lightweight enough for a child to lift.

Sturdy wooden chairs last long and are good for putting around a little table or behind a desk when serious work—like eating, reading, or writing—is involved. Make sure the seats are contoured, though; there's nothing worse for a child's concentration than an uncomfortable hardwood chair. The school-supply market offers wood chairs in many heights and styles. They've been designed for maximum comfort in the classroom, and will be just as satisfying at home.

Children often like chairs with arms so they can grab on to the sides and move themselves. "Arms also make kids feel grown-up," Ms. Pasnik says. "I'd love to see someone manufacture a child-size swivel chair with arms . . . like the ones in offices."

"Chairs with wheels are great for working because they move with the child," says Ward Bennett, "and prevent him from twisting too much. It's important to teach young people to sit

3. Youth chairs provide the extra height small children need to reach the table. This version, in natural oak with a sturdy fiber rush seat, can serve as a barstool later on. It stands 37 inches high; the outside width in front is 16½ inches and the seat height is 22 inches.

E. A. Clore Sons, Inc.: Madison, Virginia 22727 $35

4. Sun chairs bring you comfortably to baby's level. The frame is ⅞-inch round tubular aluminum with baked-enamel finish. Sleigh-runner legs give added strength on grass, sand, or other soft surfaces, so you can read in the backyard while your infant is playing. The seat is ⅝-inch-wide vinyl lattice in yellow, green, white, or brownish black. It measures 24 inches wide and sits 5½ inches from the ground.

Brown-Jordan: P.O. Box 5688, 9860 Gidley Street, El Monte, California 91734 $90

5. Not just for sitting but for slouching, right side up or upside down. A mini version of the sling, or butterfly, chair it will even hug grown-ups comfortably—although they'll have to sit up like big people. The adult version of the chair is part of the permanent design collection of the Museum of Modern Art.

The stackable frame is black wrought iron, covered with leather in a choice of eight colors. The sling, available separately, folds in quarters. Freight can add considerably to the cost of the chairs due to the bulk of the frame. When ordering, bear in mind that it saves money to ship several chairs together, since they stack so easily.

Leathercrafter: 303 East 51 Street, New York, New York 10022 $30—child's; $60—adult's

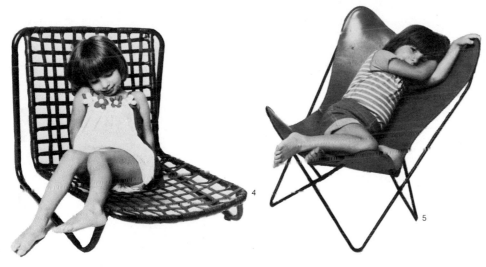

correctly right away. Secretarial-type chairs with casters are good posture chairs."

Seats without backs are great for children when they are coloring or building models. "Children aren't as concerned about leaning back as we are," Robin Berenstain explains. "They're very intense and will usually tuck a knee under their chin and lean forward." One stool on the market adjusts to a number of heights and will grow with the child; he'll be able to use it until he leaves for college. Another is a simple canvas model that's fine for watching TV or taking to the beach.

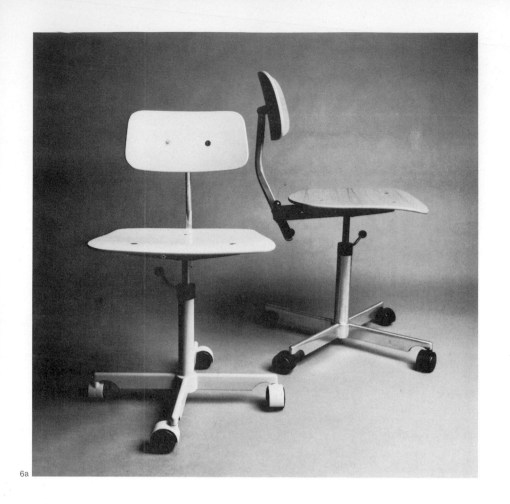

6a

6b

Chairs and stools are also a means to an end—reaching the sink, opening the refrigerator, or getting to a toy on a high shelf. A child always wants something that is beyond his reach, and he'll use a chair to get to it. And since you might prefer that he not climb on the dining room chair, a practical solution would be to get a step stool—one that you could use, too. Choose the ones that have suction devices; they stay put when weight is placed on top. One child we know is so attached to his stool that he drags it all over the house, even when he doesn't need it.

Benches invite group play because a number of kids can sit on them at the same time, all sharing the same seat. And when a bench isn't being used for sitting, it can act as a long work surface for model boats. Benches also fit well under windows so children can see what's happening outside.

6. Interior decorators consider this the ultimate desk chair for both kids and grown-ups. Its simplicity sits well in any environment, and Kevi curves just where it should to hold a five- or a fifty-year-old with equal comfort. The adjustable seat and back are molded plywood; the base is either polished or lacquered aluminum, and coasts on twin casters for maximum maneuverability and minimum wear to the floor.

The chair comes in big and little versions; the main difference between the two is the seat width. We recommend the more stable generous size (shown here), which can be raised and lowered from 14 to 19 inches. The backrest adjusts accordingly.

Kevi comes knockdown, is easily assembled, and is available in a wide choice of colors ranging from oak to yellow, black, white, and red.

Scandinavian Design: 117 East 57 Street, New York, New York 10022 $95—oak; $89—painted (dealer) Kevi A.S. Goldstrup, Denmark (mfg.)

7.

7. Appropriately called the Body Chair, this secretarial posture seat is designed to mold to the human figure. And it can hold little or big bodies because it has five comfort adjustments: a key clipped under the seat adjusts the seat height, back height, angle of the back, back tension, and seat depth.

The Fiberglas outer shell is available in matte black, beige, or brown finishes. The sculptured pedestal base is chromed steel. Choose from a wide variety of fabrics and vinyl upholstery. Cushioning is highly resilient polyurethane for even weight distribution and softness. The chair rolls on 2-inch ball-bearing casters of soft or hard rubber.

The overall height goes from 30¼ to 34¼ inches, the seat height from 18 to 20¼ inches. Overall width is 17½ inches, seat width is 17¼ inches, and seat depth is 16½ inches.

GF Business Equipment, Inc.: East Dennick Avenue, Youngstown, Ohio 44501 $242

Chairs can become playthings for imaginative children. Some are even designed to be turned upside down and thus become tables or tents. Others, made of foam, are good for bouncing or rough-and-tumble play. These chairs are generally inexpensive and good for helping a child develop creativity. Don't let a small child express his creativity by climbing on a folding chair, however; there's a chance it will collapse. Although the manufacturer says the model in this chapter won't, nothing is foolproof. We recommend it for children over eight.

Chairs and seats are not only skiddable, foldable, and adjustable; they're also lovable, rockable, and loungeable in the shape of beanbags, cubes, whistles, snake sofas, and foam hassocks. There is a seat for every child. Find the right one for yours.

8

8. Choosing the right high chair is one of the most important tasks for a new mother. Comfort and safety for the infant are vital. Independent testing labs give Cosco's chairs high marks in both. Others may be prettier, but few will serve you and your child as well.

The backrest is extra high, the seat is foam cushioned, and the positive-lock, snap-out plastic tray is large, with a substantially raised rim so spills stay put. Other key features include a sturdy, wide-stance chromed-steel frame, so you and baby will feel safe when there's a lot of movement; adjustable molded footrest; T-strap to hold the infant; and a towel bar. This model is available in different plaids and prints that change fairly often.

Cosco Home Products: 2525 State Street, Columbus, Indiana 47201 **$42.50**

9. The Tripp Trapp chair will comfortably take on toddlers, tall daddies, and short, stout grannies, depending on how the seats are positioned. Seats are held by two Z-shaped slatted pieces of beech and can be adjusted to many different heights with an Allen wrench. Tripp Trapp can start out as a high chair when used with the optional U-shaped frame to hold baby in place. Move the seat levels and it grows with the child, becoming a desk chair, a dining chair . . . even a step stool. The Norwegians, who designed it, say the adjustable footrest will encourage children to sit properly at any age. In addition to natural beech, the chair comes stained in red or brown.

Tripp Trapp Imports: 55 Ledgelawn Avenue, P.O. Box 555, Lexington, Massachusetts 02173 **$60**

9

10. Children like chairs they can use for climbing. When choosing such a chair, pay attention to how it balances under the weight of your child. This all-steel juvenile folding chair, one of the simplest around, passed our tipping tests. A great addition to the basement, den, or playroom, it closes with a single motion to fit comfortably into the front closet. Edges are fully curled to help prevent snagged clothing, and safety hinges guard against pinched fingers. Gray, blue, tan, or green baked-enamel finish. Two sizes are available: 12½-inch and 15½-inch seat heights.

Krueger: 1330 Bellevue Street, Green Bay, Wisconsin 54308 **$9.25**—juvenile; **$9.70**—junior

11. Enzo Mari designed this marvelously versatile chair for indoor or outdoor use. All the holes make the seat impervious to weather because the rain will simply slip right through them. The holes are also great for children who love to stick their fingers into everything. You can transport the chair easily since the epoxy-coated steel legs unscrew. The box-shaped seat and back are made of molded plastic in yellow, white, brown, or green. The Box Chair stands 17½ inches tall and comes unassembled in its own transparent two-handled bag.

Castelli Furniture: 950 Third Avenue, New York, New York 10022 **$40**

10a

10b

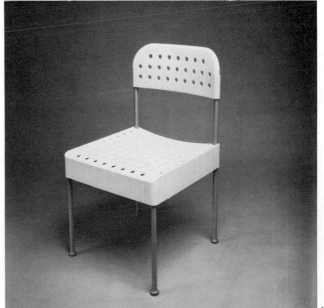

11

12a

12b

12c

12. Children like to live with lots of shapes, textures, and bright colors. These all-foam modules —besides acting as functional chairs, tables, and hassocks—are wonderful huggable play blocks. The pieces are offered in two looks: durable suede (shown here) and hide. In both cases, the core is foam, but the coating process makes the exterior either velvety or leathery. The hide look is all-purpose, featuring vinyl coverings in bold colors. Everything is stackable, washable, and, most important, flame-retardant.

The child's chair measures 19 inches long, 14 inches wide, and 17½ inches high; the cube is 15 inches; and the whistle chaise is 30 inches long, 15 inches high, and 20 inches wide.

The Carter Co.: 186 Alewipe Brook Parkway, Cambridge, Massachusetts 02138 $46—chair (suede look); $35 (hide) $35—cube (suede look); $25 (hide) $53—chaise (suede look); $42 (hide)

13. It would be hard to find someone who doesn't love sitting in a beanbag chair. Big, flexible, and floppy, beanbags move when you do—almost like playing with clay. Choose one with a sturdy covering that will stand up to rough-and-tumble activity. This one has a polypropylene-backed vinyl cover, enclosing thousands of expanded virgin polystyrene beads. There are six double-stitched panels and two zippers. It comes in a dozen earthtone colors and three sizes: pawn (84-inch diameter), queen (110-inch diameter), and king (144-inch diameter).

Bornemann Products, Inc.: 1115 West Plymouth Street, Bremen, Indiana 46505 $23, $35, and $50

14. Zippered envelopes in rich-looking tan vinyl or leather cover thousands of 3-millimeter expanded polystyrene pellets in this beanbag seat from Italy. There's no chance the seams will split when youngsters or adults repeatedly pounce on it. Dimensions are 31 by 31 by 27 inches high.

　The original sack seat was designed in 1969 and has been chosen by the Museum of Modern Art for its permanent design collection.

International Contract Furnishings, Inc.: 145 East 57 Street, New York, New York 10022 $180—vinyl; $630—leather

13

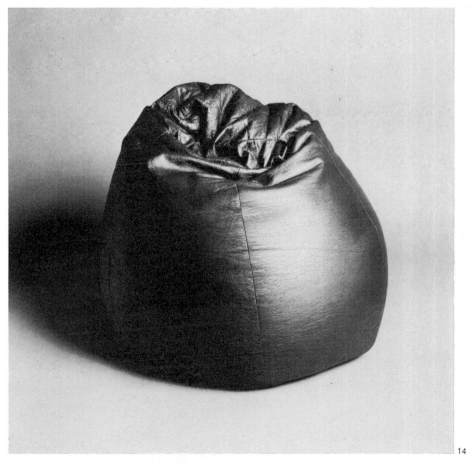

14

15.

16. **The Museum of Modern Art thought enough of this little child's chair to put it in its permanent design collection. Conceived by Marco Zanuso and Richard Sapper, it stands slightly shy of 20 inches high and has a 10-inch seat width to accommodate tiny backsides. When four or more chairs are stacked up, they make a mini play sculpture. The material is red polypropylene, and the chair legs have rubber insets to prevent skidding. A good seat for three- to five-year-olds.**

Beylerian, Ltd.: 305 East 63 Street, New York, New York 10022 $29

16. **When your child is big enough to leave the high chair and join you at the dinner table, a booster seat helps her reach the plate. It's important to choose one that draws close to the table and stays put so the tot doesn't slide around. The Bottoms Up contour-molded plastic seat by Cosco can be turned so it's either 3 or 6 inches high. You can use it as a little floor seat, too. It's washable and comes in yellow or brown.**

Cosco Home Products: 2525 State Street, Columbus, Indiana 47201 $8.50

16

17. Children love to plop
themselves down on almost
anything that will accommodate
their little bodies—orange
crates, low tables, cardboard
boxes. The seat is their
kingdom. This Stendig offering
becomes a stool, armchair, or
play table, depending on how
it's turned. Holes cut in the
sides are designed for small
hands, so tots can change the
chair's use in seconds. But
they'll probably use the cutouts
for other things...like
peepholes.

Solid birch on natural finish
with rounded edges, it'll stand
up to tough treatment in
schools or at home. Measures 12
inches all around, with a 7-inch
seat height.

Stendig, Inc.: 410 East 62 Street, New York, New York
10021 **$80**

18. **Lighter weight than the Stendig
version, this cube table/chair is
styled in laminated birch with a
clear lacquer finish. Measures
12 inches all around.**

PlayLearn Products Division, PCA Industries, Inc.: 2298
Grisson Drive, St. Louis, Missouri 63141 **$23**

17

18

19.

20.

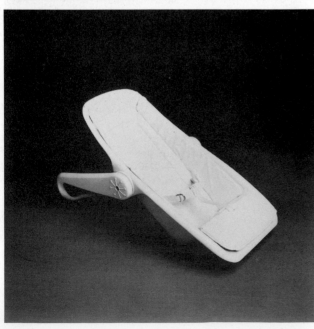

21.

19. Some baby nurses claim the kitchen sink is the best place to bathe baby. Its self-contained drain and proximity to counter space are definite pluses. By comparison, portable molded plastic tubs and inflatable ones presently on the market are small and quickly outgrown. Bathinettes are cumbersome, short-lived for the money, and a nuisance to fill and drain.

The largest portable tub we could find is part of a bathinette but can be purchased separately. It is 30 inches long by 16 inches wide and features a hammock for infants who can't yet sit. Later, you can remove the hammock and place it right in the big bath so your toddler will feel more secure. The tub does not fit close to the faucet in standard-size baths, so a hose or container will be necessary to fill it.

Pride Trimble Corp.: P.O. Box 431, Burbank, California 91503 $10

20. Many parents will prefer this white molded plastic toilette for toilet training because it looks like the real thing. During the first training stages, children feel secure putting their feet on solid ground; besides, the floor provides the necessary "push" and foot support for good bowel action. Later on, the seat and lid can be detached and placed on the regular toilet.

The base is flared for good stability. There's a removable receptacle and pliable deflector.

Cosco Home Products: 2525 State Street, Columbus, Indiana 47201 $8

21. A portable baby carrier is a staple in every infant's wardrobe and one of the first things a new mother needs. Basically, all carriers are designed so that the baby can sleep or play and still be within view while mother works around the house. Cosco's Cradelette features a white plastic molded shell with a safety strap and a sturdy molded arm that rotates to any position, then clicks into place.

The vinyl-covered foam pad can be removed for cleaning or replacement.

Cosco Home Products: 2525 State Street, Columbus, Indiana 47201 **$14**

22. When you've had enough running for the day, a walker will keep baby occupied, erect, and secure. That way, the infant can zoom around after you. Most walkers are collapsible; this one isn't. Although it may not be a great space saver, its solid polypropylene body will protect the child from bumps and knocks and the cone shape will keep harmful objects out of reach. Ball-bearing casters move wherever little legs want and help a child walk easily over any surface.

Pines of America, Inc.: 5120 Investment Drive, Fort Wayne, Indiana 46808 **$20**

22

23. Here's a walker that collapses flat to save space. Features include a tip-resistant wide-stance base, padded vinyl bucket seat with high back support, and covered joints to prevent pinching. Good quality ball casters help the child move smoothly over the carpet. The seat and tray section adjusts to twenty different positions to assure your finding the exact height for your infant.

Century Products, Inc.: 2150 West 114 Street, Cleveland, Ohio 44102 **$26**

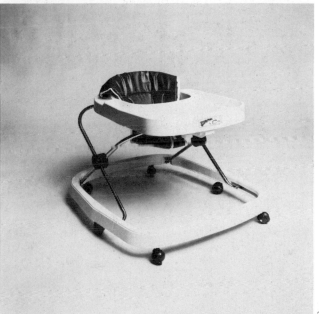

23

24. Infants as young as four weeks can be put in this sleeper/bouncer/walker because it has a three-position reclining back-rest. When the back is completely flat, tiny babies can nap. An adjustable spring lets you increase the tension as the child grows and gets heavier. The vinyl seat is padded with fire-retardant polyfoam and comes solid or printed. There's a rubber-coated wire bumper and heavy-duty white plastic play tray. Recommended for children up to eighteen months.

Frank F. Taylor Co.: Box 636, Frankfort, Kentucky 40602 **$25**

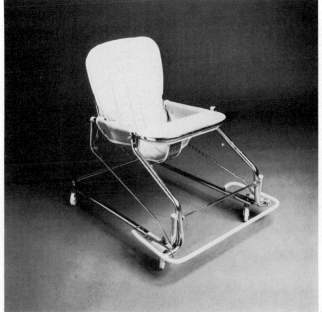

24

25a

25b

25. Put six children on a bench and they'll all start talking and playing together. Benches invite socializing—they're places where lots of people can relax without the barriers of arms. They are the center of activity in parks and playgrounds, baseball stadiums, football arenas, schoolyards, and gymnasiums.

Park a bench at home—or a set of three nesting benches. When your child has friends over, they can play school. And if no one else happens to be around, the benches make a wonderful play center by themselves.

Stendig's set of three, in birch plywood with red or yellow lacquered seats, features solid birch rounded legs. If you don't want the whole set, you can buy just one. The low unit is 51¼ inches long, 10 inches deep, and 7½ inches high. The middle piece is 59 inches long, 12½ inches deep, and 11 inches high. And the mother bench is 66¾ inches long, 14½ inches deep, and 23½ inches high, with a 14½-inch seat height and a double rail back.

Stendig, Inc.: 410 East 62 Street, New York, New York 10021 $600—the set; $300—large alone; $190—medium; $155—small

26. Looking as if it came in from the park, this contoured bench is 48 inches long and made of treated pine slats. Used outdoors or in, it will certainly invite kids to climb all over it.

Algoma Net Co.: 310 Fourth Street, Algoma, Wisconsin 54201 $50

26

27. Another bench to pull up alongside a child's worktable or play table. Lyon's model is certainly more industrial-looking than Stendig's, but is just as adaptable. Actually designed for locker-room wear and tear, it features a seat in selected hardwood with a clear plastic sealer and an enameled steel base . . . sturdy enough for kids who want to play gym at home. Measures 9½ inches wide by 18 inches high. Available in lengths starting at 5 feet 10 inches (shown here) and going up to 9 feet 10 inches.

Lyon Metal Products, Inc.: P.O. Box 671, Aurora, Illinois 60507 **$88 to $140**

28. Still another bench offering, this clean-looking portable unit has an aluminum surface on steel pipe legs that are capped in red rubber. Measures 6 feet by 10 inches, and can be used for outdoor play as well.

PlayLearn Products Division, PCA Industries, Inc.: 2298 Grisson Drive, St. Louis, Missouri 63141 **$63**

27

28

29

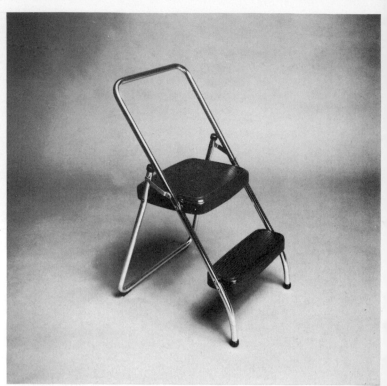

31

30

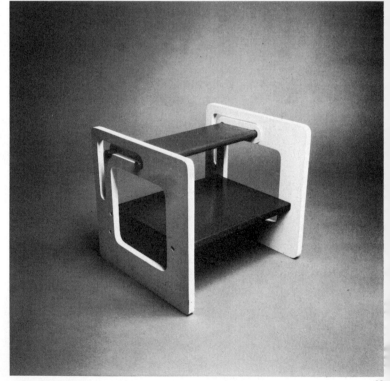

32

9. In addition to providing a safe way to raid the cookie jar or reach a high shelf, this 14-inch stool is meant to be kicked around. It rolls on spring-loaded casters right to where it's wanted. Step on top; the casters retract and the rubber base ring firmly grabs the floor and locks. The Kik-Step from Cramer Industries is made of heavy-gauge steel with baked-enamel finish in a wide variety of colors, including ebony, fire-engine red, white, yellow, and beige. The double platform has a ribbed rubber tread.

Cramer Industries, Inc.: 625 Adams Street, Kansas City, Missouri 66105 $40

0. This 13-inch-high stool has an extra little step for kids who want to rest their bottoms on top and their feet on the bottom. Made of heavy-duty molded plastic, it has retractable casters and anti-skid ring, which let the stool move easily or sit firmly in place. Rubbermaid has designed it in gold, orange, beige, or black.

Rubbermaid Commercial Products, Inc.: 3124 Valley Avenue, Winchester, Virginia 22601 $20

1. Another step stool that's ideal for sink reaching, this one automatically folds to 4¾ inches flat when you lift the handle, so it can be put out of the way when space is at a premium. Enamel-trimmed steps are 8½ and 17 inches high. Legs are chrome. Comes in yellow or chocolate brown.

Cosco Home Products: 2525 State Street, Columbus, Indiana 47201 $19

33

34

34 & 35

32. The activity chair performs four functions, so your children will probably love it. Depending on how the backrest is positioned within the L-shaped opening, this can be a regular little seat, a step stool for tots who want to reach a high toy shelf, a floor desk for the crayon contingent, or a higher chair when turned over. It's made of wood and painted in bright red or yellow and white.

Nursery Originals, Inc.: 280 Rand Street, Central Falls, Rhode Island 02863 $18

33. Mothers can soothe baby or just sit back and relax in this large hardwood and pine rocker. The taped back provides extra comfort and is available in a wide choice of beautiful muted colors. The rocker comes in kit form with hardware, glue, light or dark stains, and tape for the seat and back. It's simple to assemble and is a true reproduction of a classic Shaker design. Height is 42 inches, width across arm 25 inches, and depth 19 inches.

Shaker Workshop, Inc.: Concord, Massachusetts 01742 $100

34. An old Shaker style, this child's rocker is made of selected northern hardwoods and pine, with a woven tape seat. Like most Shaker Workshop pieces, it comes in kit form with hardware, glue, light or dark stains, and tape. It is easy to assemble; no special workshop tools are necessary. The height of the back is 29 inches, the width is 15 inches, and the depth is 11½ inches.

Shaker Workshop, Inc.: Concord, Massachusetts 01742 $35

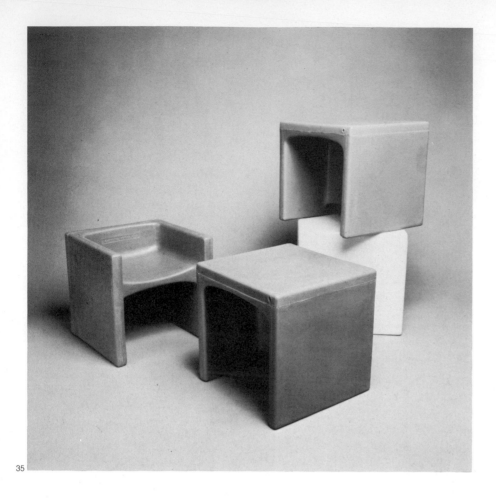

35.

36.

35. One of the most wonderful things about very young people is their ability to create fantasy worlds around themselves with the simplest objects. A cube, the most elemental shape, can be used to build cars, trains, boats, even bathtubs. These 15-inch molded plastic Educubes also serve as chairs, desks, and step stools when the imagination wanes. Adults can use them as end tables, plant stands, or hassocks. There are four to a set—red, blue, yellow, and green.

Learning Products, Inc.: 11632 Fairgrove Industrial Boulevard, St. Louis, Missouri 63043 **$85**—set of four

36. These are colorful, fun chairs that even the smallest three-year-old will fit into and appreciate. They are of light-weight one-piece construction with rounded surfaces. After a birthday party or other social occasion, simply wipe them clean and stack; the nonstatic thermoplastic surface doesn't attract dust.

There's a 12-inch seat height for three- to six-year-olds and a 13½-inch height for the older set, seven through twelve. Available in white, yellow, red, or orange—colors children love.

Krueger: 1330 Bellevue Street, Green Bay, Wisconsin 54308 **$26.50**—either size

37. There's something to be said for chairs that are just plain durable—simple, well-constructed pieces for the nursery, playroom, or study. Fiberglas is one of the most sturdy compositions. It will even take crayon scribbles, which can easily be wiped off with a damp cloth. Krueger's Fiberglas chairs come in a variety of widths, heights, and depths, ranging from a 23⅜-inch seat height for first graders to a 32¼-inch height for adults. Extended rear legs keep the backrest from scraping the walls. The chairs also stack, and they feature leg glides so the floor doesn't get unnecessarily marred. The

company offers an optional bookrack—great for kids who never know where they put their math books. Colors range from brick red to white, with chrome or black enamel legs.

Krueger: 1330 Bellevue Street, Green Bay, Wisconsin 54308 $27.20—23⅜ inches; $32.00—32¼ inches

37

38

38. Plastic chairs can last a lifetime, and if you pick the right one, you may love it that long. The late Joe Colombo designed his stack chair more than a decade ago and it's become a classic, behind a desk or at the dinner table. The colors are green, red, white, and cordovan and the price is reasonable. Seat is 16¾ inches wide and 16 inches high; height is 28 inches overall.

Beylerian, Ltd.: 305 East 63 Street, New York, New York 10022 $35

39. When the entire house is carpeted, your youngster needs a chair that glides without too much trouble. This model has a horizontal sled base that will slide equally well over carpeting and resilient flooring. It features a one-piece contoured shell of nylon or high-impact plastic with a square tubular steel frame in chrome or matte black. Comes in black, gold, blue, green, bronze, or red in five sizes, with 12- to 17½-inch seat heights for preschool through high school kids.

American Seating: 901 Broadway Avenue N.W., Grand Rapids, Michigan 49504 $20—all sizes

39

40a

40b

41

40. Little kids often love to watch while mommy tends to the newborn. Invite your three-year-old to sit nearby in his own little folding chair while you feed the baby in a rocker. Both pieces are handcrafted from New England hardwood and varnished rawhide. The 34-inch-high rocker has a 17-inch seat height and makes a lovely comfortable place to lull baby to sleep. The folding chair is 28 inches overall with an 8-inch seat height. When the weather is nice, the weather-resistant urethane finish lets you take the chairs outside. They come knockdown for easy shipping. The snowshoe rocker and canoe chair are also available in cane for less.

Vermont Tubbs, Inc.: Forestdale, Vermont 05745 $100 —rocker; $65—folding chair

41. Harry Bertoia, designer of the classic chair collection bearing his name, said his pieces are "mostly made of air ... space passes right through them." His child's chair has a gently curved fused-finish welded-steel wire seat and back with a welded-steel rod base. Kids can crawl all over it, play peekaboo, be sloppy, and not hurt the sculptured piece at all. The seat is covered with a fully upholstered foam pad. Chair and cushion come in a variety of colors plus black and white. Measures 15¾ inches wide, 16¼ inches deep, and 24 inches high.

Knoll International, Inc.: 745 Fifth Avenue, New York, New York 10022 $92—chair; $20—pad

42. A trio of cane stools for kids of all sizes. They'll drag them all over the place to watch themselves in the mirror or stare at you while you're preparing dinner. The big stool is 20 by 12 inches and the baby stool is 10 by 9 inches.

India Nepal: 233 Fifth Avenue, New York, New York 10016 $35—the set

43. This lightweight pocket chair is designed to take to parks, campsites, beaches, and a day at the potato races. But it might be fun to keep it right at home, where your child can use it in front of the TV or by a tree. Constructed of hard steel wire with a canvas seat in stripes or solid red or blue, it folds to pocket size, so you can put it in a drawer when the day is over. Children love walking around with the seat tucked under their backsides, sitting whenever and wherever they want. Measures 7½ by 14 by 14 inches.

Champion Industries: 35 East Poplar Street, Philadelphia, Pennsylvania 19123 $6

44. Some hunters do a lot of sitting and need chairs that are comfortable and strong, but at the same time lightweight and easy to move. This hunter's chair meets all of those qualifications, but can also be part of your child's equipment even if he's not a professional sportsman. It would be great at the beach, on a hike, or by the creek when he's fishing.

The lightweight 1-inch aluminum tube frame is strong and the U-shaped leg construction provides good support. The back and seat are made of olive drab duck with double sewn seams, and can be removed for washing. A gear bag attached to the seat has a heavy-duty zipper and will hold bait, bathing suits, or sandwiches. Your kids can grab the chair by the carrying strap— and away they go. Available in 18- or 19-inch heights.

Tucker Duck and Rubber Co.: 2701 Kelley Highway, P.O. Box 4167, Fort Smith, Arkansas 72914 $15

42

43

44

153

45a

45. **Alvar Aalto** furniture has been around since the early thirties, when it was designed by the Finnish architect. It's the kind of no-nonsense seating that can be passed on to your children's children and never look tired. Constructed of sturdy birch with rounded turns, Alvar Aalto furnishings are preferred by the Finnish and Swedish governments for their schools. The stool has a solid seat edged by a smooth band. The four legs are also solid wood—sliced, bent, and then glued into place. The stool stacks, and makes a great play seat that can easily be tucked into a corner when space is at a premium. After the kids have outgrown it as a play piece, it works well as an end table or snack table. The chair is also stackable and has a comfortable curved backrest. Prices are on the high side, but the value and looks are there.

International Contract Furnishings, Inc.: 145 East 57 Street, New York, New York 10022 $67—stool; $95—chair

45 b

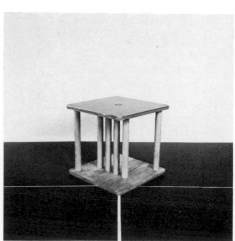

46

46. A series of wood dowels is set in between two 16-inch squares of polyurethaned overlaid birch plywood. Turn it one way and it's an end table or stool; turn it so the squares are vertical and it's a little chair. Kids will respond to its versatility and will love dropping things through the holes in the sides. The dowels make it easy to lift. This two-chair table cube comes natural or painted in red, blue, yellow, or green. All corners are rounded for safe sitting.

Placewares: 13 Walden Street, Concord, Massachusetts 01742 $36

47

47. This is a chair kids can stand on. Its solid rounded birch legs are placed at extreme corners, and the stretchers are strategically set so that it's difficult to overturn. Geometrically shaped to look good behind a desk or sit alone in the corner of a room, the chair comes in four sizes: 14½ inches wide and 13½ inches deep by 20¼, 22¼, or 24½ inches high, or 15¾ inches wide, 16 inches deep, and 29 inches high. Seat heights are 11, 13, 14½, and 16¼ inches. The seat surface is red or yellow and finished with a nontoxic satin lacquer, which wipes clean with a damp sponge.

Stendig, Inc.: 410 East 62 Street, New York, New York 10021 $82 to $103

48. When toddlers start getting together in small groups, call on chairs they can call their own. Community Playthings, which has been designing children's nursery and kindergarten equipment for years, believes in sturdiness and offers these stackable maple toddler chairs with plywood backs. The front legs are braced with dowels that also accommodate little feet and legs. The sides and arms hold the child securely.

The seat is 9 or 12 inches high, 10 inches wide, and 8⅝ inches deep.

Community Playthings: Rifton, New York 12471 $20—9 inches; $21—12 inches

48

49. Secretaries use this stool when they want to reach low files comfortably. Kids will love its portability. It is 14 inches high, rolls on 2-inch rubber casters, and has a hardwood seat. The base is gray steel.

Hallowell Division, Standard Pressed Steel Co.: Township Line Road, Hatfield, Pennsylvania 19440 $35

50. Cater to kids' ups and downs when it comes to seating. Doing homework at a desk and gluing together a model plane at the kitchen counter require separate seating levels. This stool is equipped with a height-changing mechanism that kids love to play with. Use it in several spots as a utility chair. We're showing chrome-plated metal and black lacquered versions, but the stool comes in six other colors, too. There is a variety of optional accessories, including ball-bearing casters, foot rings, backrests, and pullover seat cushions.

Choose from two seat height adjustments—16 inches to 21 inches, and 19 inches to 27 inches—depending on your needs. A general rule of thumb is to subtract 12 inches from the height of the work surface to find a mid-range adjustment point on the stool. The 19- to 27-inch height should have a ring to rest feet on.

Ajusto Equipment Co.: 20163 Haskins Road, Bowling Green, Ohio 43402 $51—chrome; $37—black and colors; $8—casters

51. This beautifully constructed lacquered beechwood kindergarten chair has a solid seat and sturdy back. Four plastic buffers will prevent marring of the floor when your child gets restless and decides to cart the chair around the room. The round legs are glued into the oval seat, which stands 11¼ inches high. There are also two larger versions available: 12½ and 13⅔ inches.

American Montessori Society: 150 Fifth Avenue, New York, New York 10011 $30—all sizes

49

50a

50b

52. Remember the wooden chairs you used to squirm in and sit on in grade school? You knew which was yours by the scratches. Those sturdy seats got pushed and dragged but never wore out. They're still around, functional as ever, behind a desk or in front of the TV. Appalachian oak is the wood. Seats are expansion-free and saddled to make sitting comfortable—maybe even more so at home than at school.

We've chosen three seat heights to show: 10, 12, and 14 inches. The size you pick depends, of course, on the size of your scholar. Also available with study arms.

Standard School Equipment Co.: Siler City, North Carolina 27344 $20—10 inches; $23—12 and 14 inches

53. Originally designed over one hundred years ago, this child's rocker is basic enough to fit into either a traditional or a modern setting. Shown here in natural oak with a fiber rush seat, it's a children's classic. Those with more traditional tastes can choose walnut, cherry, or maple. The width of the chair between the arms in front is 14½ inches.

Then, when a tot wants to rest his feet, he can do it on a matching natural oak stool. Little people also love to drag small stools from room to room so they can sit and watch dad shaving or mom paying the bills. After their favorite TV show, they can easily pick up the stool and take it to the next center of activity. The stool measures 10 by 14 inches, with 10- or 12-inch post heights. It also welcomes grown-up feet.

E. A. Clore Sons, Inc.: Madison, Virginia 22727 $35—rocker; $10—stool

54. Straight-backed oak chairs that look as if they came out of a Quaker schoolroom have seats constructed of shaped slats. Available in 10-, 12-, and 14-inch seat heights.

Community Playthings: Rifton, New York 12471 $14.00 —10 and 12 inches; $14.50—14 inches

51

53

52

54

Lighting & Accessories

By now you may have decided you want three new storage units, five different chairs, a big portable worktable, a kid's tent, a sleeping bag, and an ice cream maker. But before you send for the catalogs, we want you to see a few more items we think are pretty special. We're calling them accessories because they really can't be categorized any other way. Many of them—for example, the sterling silver teething ring—would make wonderful baby gifts; others you'll want to keep for yourself.

The items, as you'll see, range from a charming night-light shaped like a goose to a sleek non-breakable mirror. We've chosen each one with the idea that it will add a little something to your child's environment: a bit of flair or even a touch of practicality. They aren't just good-looking and well designed; every piece has a function. For instance, children should have globes because they're the best geography teachers around. And what better way to learn to tell time than by a real clock with big bold numbers?

The most important environmental accessories are lights. The selection here is small, but we think it covers every need. There are clip-on desk lights, night-lights, lights that hang from the ceiling or walls, lights that are fixed to the bed's headboard or stand on the floor. Different types of lighting can create islands of comfort for children. One overhead fixture, while okay for general illumination, isn't much good for doing homework at a desk or painting at an easel. Local lighting provides emphasis on different activities and gives clarity to small-scaled children's tasks.

One wall light set in a corner of a room can create a cozy reading environment with the addition of a small bookshelf and comfortable chair. If two children are in a room—one doing homework and the other quietly playing—a small desk lamp can spotlight the homework while the rest of the room stays moderately lit. That way the working child will not be too distracted. Local lighting, however, should never be much brighter than the remainder of the room or else it will create gloominess.

Shaded lamps, which take up valuable space, usually manage to get in the way and interrupt the movement of work or play. Flexible lights that move up, down, or sideways are better because they can concentrate pools of light where you want them. One portable floor fixture that can be moved throughout the room can also define an activity. whether it's taking place in bed or on the floor. Track lighting, according to most

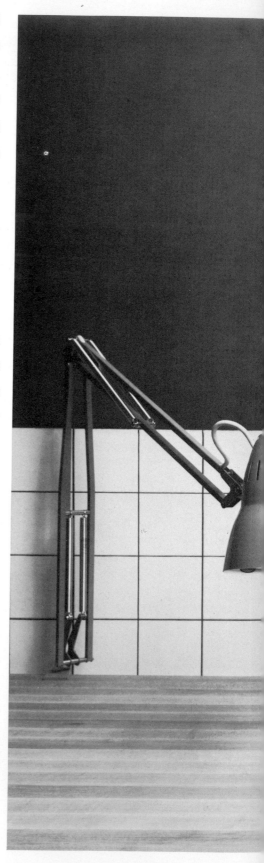

1. Architects and designers love Luxo lamps because they move in all directions, don't overheat, fit handsomely into any environment, and can either be clamped to tables, attached to walls, or stand on floor and table bases.

Clockwise: The Bullet has an adjustable arm with 4⅝-inch diameter bullet shade, inner reflector, and porcelain socket. One model has a 45-inch reach and another a 30-inch reach. Each comes with a clamp for mounting to horizontal surfaces. Available only in gray.

The Headlight is designed to be mounted directly to a wall or, with its removable pressure clip in place, to a headboard. Swivel it to wherever you want to shed some light on the subject. All-metal construction and baked-enamel finish in black, white, red, yellow, or brown.

Luxo Lil is a little lamp that fits almost anywhere, a high-intensity light with a vented double shade that assures a cool touch. This one has a 24-inch reach, cushioned, heavyweighted base, and a tension control knob to adjust movement. Available with optional brackets for attaching to horizontal or vertical surfaces. Chrome, black, yellow, white, red, or brown.

Model L has an adjustable arm with 6¾-inch diameter classic shade, inner reflector, and porcelain socket. One model has a 45-inch reach and another a 30-inch reach. This light can be wall- or table-mounted. The 45-inch model is available in tan, oyster, black, and gray; 30-inch in gray only.

Luxo Lamp Corp.: Monument Park, Port Chester, New York 10573 $45—Bullet; $23—Headlight; $36—Luxo Lil (painted); $80—Luxo Lil (chrome); $46—Luxo L; $75—T-Stand

2

3

2. Designed to provide surveillance for large areas or to prevent accidents at intersections, detection mirrors also prove handy at home. They come flat or convex, with 18- to 36-inch diameters. Although the convex surface reflects a larger area, the flat style is better for those who want a distortion-free image. Features for both styles include laminated safety glass, all-steel installation hardware and backing, and a black rubber rim. The mirror can be installed easily on the wall or ceiling, and it adjusts to any viewing angle on its all-steel ball swivel. Any girl would love one above her vanity for combing her hair or applying makeup.

Bell Glass & Mirror Co.: 1328 Flatbush Avenue, Brooklyn, New York 11210 $60—18 inches (convex); $100—18 inches (flat); $129—36 inches (convex); $175—36 inches (flat)

3. It won't break because it's not glass, but this mirror's chrome-plated steel surface will reflect just as well. The satin chrome-finished frame attaches flush to the wall with flat screws so young people can't get hurt by protruding corners. Two overall sizes: 10 1/16 by 11 3/16 inches, or 12 1/2 by 16 1/2 inches.

Folger Adam Co.: 700 Railroad Street, Joliet, Illinois 60436 $26 and $56

4. Big 18-wheel trucks have these West Coast mirrors so the drivers can clearly see what's happening all around them. They got their name because the trucks usually travel from coast to coast. The mirrors are handsome enough to go on a wall and big enough for good viewing. It might even be fun to attach one to an open shelving unit so the kids can primp and groom.

Measuring 6 inches by 14 1/2 inches, this mirror is finished in a black powder coating. Arms are telescopic so the mirror can easily be moved in and out.

Yankee Metal Products Corp.: 25 Grand Street, Norwalk, Connecticut 06852 $50 (6 by 14 1/2 inches)

architects and designers, is ideal for general illumination because the different components can be fixed to shine in different directions at the same time.

Dimmers are great because they provide variation in the light levels. The lights can be turned way up when the children are climbing on gym equipment or turned down low for TV watching. "Children should learn about rheostats at an early age," says designer Ward Bennett. Fluorescent lighting is generally harsh and certainly not recommended for infants. Soft incandescent light is best. A light can also provide color in a room. Luxo lamps come in beautiful bright colors and look striking against neutral walls.

Night-lights can often soothe a child who's afraid of the dark. Or think of laying a flashlight by your child's bedside to help him get to the bathroom in the middle of the night. But the best light of all, of course, is often daylight—so if you've got the windows, let it in.

5

6

7

5. Casters can be attached to almost any piece of furniture when you desire mobility. Frequently designed for industrial, commercial, and institutional applications, they also come more highly styled.

Generally, casters with bigger wheels and harder treads will roll and swivel more easily on carpeting and take heavier loads. Soft rubber wheels are better for smooth hardwood floors.

Casters are available in all sizes with a variety of features. Once you've decided where you want to attach them, you can determine which model will do the best job.

Shepherd Products U.S. Inc.: 203 Kerth Street, St. Joseph, Michigan 49085 1½-inches to 5-inch diameters—$5.30 to $15 for sets of four

Bassick Division, Stewart Warner Corp.: 960 Atlantic Street, Bridgeport, Connecticut 06604 1-inch to 5-inch diameters—$1 to $20 for single casters

6. Remind Brian to do his homework by pinning a note to the refrigerator door with a magnetic clip. This one will really hold lots of papers without sliding off. The clip opens full and has heavy chrome plating. It comes in a few sizes, starting with 1³⁄₁₆ by 1⅜ by ¾ inches.

Wescosa, Inc.: P.O. Box 66626, 62 Mt. Hermon Road, Scotts Valley, California 95066 $.95—small; $1.70—medium; $2.50—large

7. Nylon hardware is supposedly better than plastic—easier to clean, nonstatic, and more durable. This collection consists of recessed poles for cabinet doors, knobs, and arc-shaped drawer pulls.

Forms and Surfaces: P.O. Box 5215, Santa Barbara, California 93108 $2.65 to $3.55

8. Besides looking good, soft-rubber hardware won't hurt when a youngster runs into a door. The material used is neoprene and it's been fashioned into drawer pulls, door stops, clothes hooks, and finger poles.

Forms and Surfaces: P.O. Box 5215, Santa Barbara, California 93108 prices range from $2.60 for a knob to $4.85 for the clothes hook

9

10

9. Clocks with lines instead of numbers may be attractive, but they won't be much good for teaching how to tell time. This clock not only has large numbers to show the hours, but small ones to indicate the minutes. There's also a red sweep second hand. It may have your two-year-old counting to sixty in no time at all.

Housing comes in bronze, chrome, painted steel, or aluminum. A painted model, in red, orange, blue, tan, or sunflower, is a wonderful way to add color to a child's room. Battery- or cord-operated.

Peter Pepper Products, Inc.: 17929 South Susana Road, Compton, California 90221 $53—electric (solid colors); $65—electric (chrome); $69—battery (solid colors); $81—battery (chrome)

10. Many offices and factories use this wall clock because the black numerals are easy to read against the white background. The case comes in tan or chrome metal. The small version has an 8-inch dial, the larger model a 12-inch dial.

Seth Thomas Division of General Time Corp.: 135 South Main Street, Thomaston, Connecticut 06787 $18—tan; $20—chrome

11. Clothes don't have to rest only on hangers and be stashed in some closet. Try cleats. They're sensible, good-looking alternatives that can hang right out in the open. Generally used on boat decks to hold the boat to the dock with rope, cleats can support lots of weight at home. A few hung vertically in the bath can hold towels and robes; some in the foyer would be

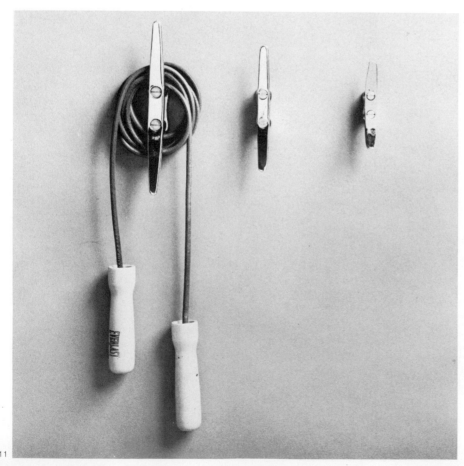

11

great for coats, hats, even umbrellas; a bunch in the bedroom can take on shirts and sweaters. These are chrome-plated, and although they cost more than hangers, they'll serve you well. Lengths range from 3½ inches to 8 inches.

Goldbergs Marine: 202 Market Street, Philadelphia, Pennsylvania 19106 $3 (3½ inches); $7.50 (8 inches).

12. One of the best teachers your children can have, a globe will show them how big the world really is. Instead of telling a bedtime story, try pointing out a country and talking about the people who live there. This model has a 12-inch diameter, the size used in many classrooms. Raised relief lets the child feel the mountains. Countries are shown in contrasting colors to emphasize their sizes and shapes. Gyro mounting makes it easy to swing the globe up or down to bring any area into view. Routes can then be easily wiped off. The base and axis are gray metal, available also in goldtone.

Replogle Globes: 1901 North Narragansett Avenue, Chicago, Illinois 60639 $25

13. A big map can help your youngster learn the difference between New York and Ohio and might also give her an appreciation of our nation's vastness. This four-color United States map would look great hanging on a wall. It's vinyl-coated paper, so that travel routes can be marked on with crayon and then wiped off. Comes with bass wood rods at the top and bottom and metal tab hangers. Measures 61 by 52 inches; one inch represents 50 miles. A more expensive map on a spring roller is also available. There are world maps, too, for the bigger picture.

Modern School Equipment Co.: 524 East Jackson, Goshen, Indiana 46526 $30

12

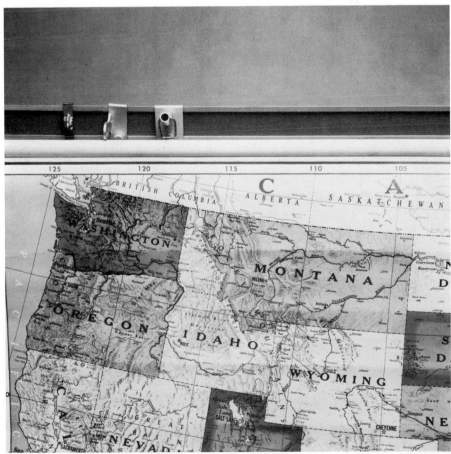

13

167

14.

14. Children produce a profuse amount of vibrant, fresh, and wonderful artwork, often worthy of framing. Many parents love to show off their children's best efforts by hanging them throughout the house. A good quality frame can give a surprisingly professional finish. Frames are available in a wide range of materials and prices, but since you're getting the art free, you might want to consider spending more on the frame for a quality look. Kulicke Frames, Inc. does a lot of custom work for famous artists and museums throughout the country, but also carries a line of standard size do-it-yourself frames. The ones shown here represent some of the most popular styles.

Clockwise:

Metal Section Frame comes in lengths from 5 inches to 40 inches. Two packs make up a complete frame that can be assembled in minutes. Available in aluminum, gold, or colors.

$6.60—pack of 16-inch lengths; $7.70—20 inches

Aluminum Total Frame includes everything you need except the picture—backing, mat board, conservation paper, and clear acrylic. It comes in silver, gold, black, white, or red. Sizes go up from 5 by 7 inches to 24 by 30 inches.

$9.00 to $33.00

Woodline O Frame (center) is available in light ash or dark walnut wood. Sizes start at 9 by 12 inches and go to 24 by 30 inches.

$12.00 to $38.50 (ash); $15.00 to $40.00 (walnut)

Trap Frame picture is sandwiched between two sheets of clear acrylic and held with bands of clear plastic or polished aluminum in silver, gold, or bronze. Sizes run from 6 by 8 inches to 24 by 30 inches.

$15.40 to $71.00

Collection Box Frame is a clear plastic wraparound frame with a glossy white box insert. There's a half-inch space inside the frame to display collections of

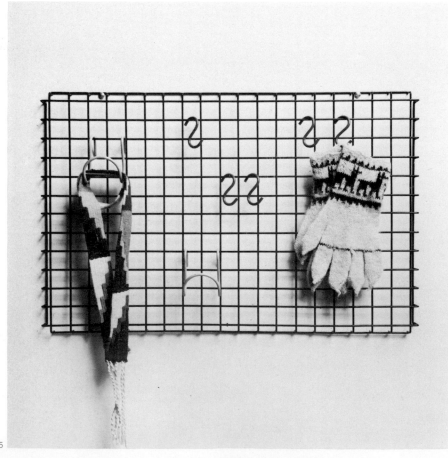

15

shells, coins, or flowers.
Available in sizes from 5 by 7
inches to 11 by 14 inches.
$6.00 to $13.00
Box Frame, similar to the
Collection Box, is ideal for
prints, photos, or maps. Sizes
run from 5 by 7 inches to 16 by
20 inches.
$4.00 to $19.00
Kulicke Frames, Inc.: 636 Broadway, New York, New York
10012

15. Towels, kitchen utensils, toys, or
tools would look striking
hanging on this simple black
metal grille. It comes from Italy
and is available with double,
single, S, and clip hooks. Three
sizes: 5½ inches by 36 inches, 18
by 27½, and 36 by 27½.
Placewares: 13 Walden Street, Concord, Massachusetts
01742 $8.50, $13.95, and $22.00

16. The Shakers stressed simplicity
and clean design in everything
they built. Their peg hangers
can become one of the easiest
ways to unclutter a room today.
Hats, chairs, toys, can all hang
neatly on these well-styled oak
expanses. There are a number
of lengths ranging from 12 to 36
inches.
Shaker Workshop, Inc.: Concord, Massachusetts 01742
$4—12 inches; $8—36 inches

17. Some more boards to help get
things out of the way. Available
in white oak with one to eight
turned oak pegs.
Charles Webb: 28 Church Street, Cambridge,
Massachusetts 02138 $14—7 inches; $26—28 inches;
$42—52 inches

18. Some kids think it's easier to
take their clothes off the hanger
than it is to put them back on.
They might be neater if their
belongings hung on colorful
plastic junior hangers that look
like toys. Each measures 12 by 9
inches with an upper hook that
sits on any size closet rod. A
rainbow of colors including red,
blue, green, and orange; or
white or crystal.
Wings Over the World Corp.: 225 Fifth Avenue, New York,
New York 10010 $1.25; $7.50—set of six

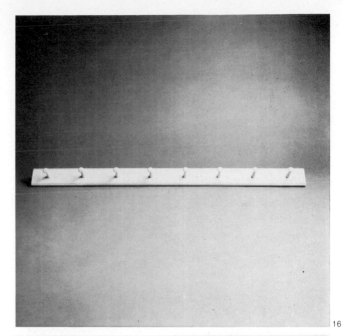

16

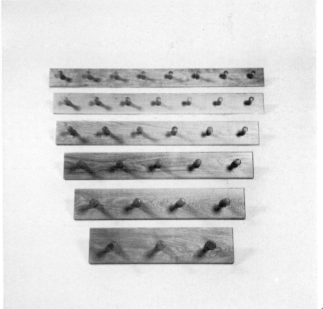

17

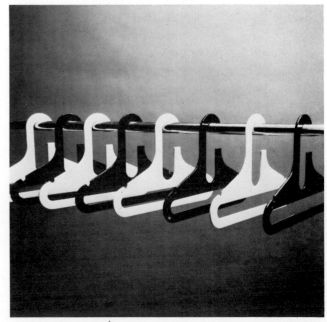

18

19.

19. Crazy as it sounds, this salad dryer can also take most of the water from wet nylons. Put them in the basket, spin the top, and the stockings come out almost water-free. It will come in handy for your college daughter who is down to her last pair of pantyhose. The cover, drain basket, and bowl are made of polypropylene. The dryer also does a fine job on lettuce, vegetables, fruit, and berries.

Mouli Manufacturing Corp.: 1 Montgomery Street, Belleville, New Jersey 07109 **$13**

20. Everyone remembers the humidifier mother put in the bedroom during cold season and how it made it much easier to breathe. Even when no one has a cold, a humidifier is great for your family as well as your furniture. Many hospitals prefer Walton's cold steam humidifier, the Squire. It's considered a high-quality professional product that will produce 5 gallons of moisture a day. That's enough to humidify up to five rooms at once for twelve hours. Put it in the hall outside the bedrooms and the whole family will wake up feeling good. Designed for a long life with an all-metal construction and solid brass and copper working parts, the Squire can be cleaned and reused year after year. It has an on-off switch and grounded electrical cord. The company also makes a tabletop model that will produce 2½ gallons of humidity a day for smaller spaces.

Walton Laboratories: 1 Carol Place, Moonachie, New Jersey 07074 **$130**—Squire; **$100**—Knight

20.

21. Children don't have to go to bed with wet heads if you've got one of those fast-working hair dryers. Weighing only 10 ounces, this mini model is 5 inches long and 2⅛ inches wide. It has 1,000-watt power, so it will work quickly even on long hair, and it's small enough to fit into your child's backpack for a trip to grandma's house. Styled in white with bright red graphics, it looks pretty hanging right out in the open.

Norelco Consumer Products Divisions: 100 East 42 Street, New York, New York 10017 $14.95

22. Every new mother worries about whether she'll hear the baby crying when she's out of earshot. The Baby-Com intercom system lets you listen continuously to sounds in the nursery. A miniature radio transmitter, it operates with an AM radio, which can be placed up to 300 feet from the unit. Its portability and uncomplicated installation are also a plus; you can take it along to grandma's with ease when she's baby-sitting over the weekend.

Fanon-Courier Corp., Resdel Industries: 990 South Fairoaks Avenue, Pasadena, California 91105 $18

21

22

171

23

23. Plump bear sits on top of a sterling silver rattle (left). It's cool to teething gums and will even look good covered with tiny tooth marks. It's something that makes an endearing gift.

Even babies who weren't born with silver spoons in their mouths will enjoy the sterling silver teething ring (right). And it will probably be something special long after the child stops using it. Available with six different animals, it also comes as a pendant (center), which can be used as a Christmas tree ornament.

Cazenovia Abroad, Ltd.: 67 Albany Street, Cazenovia, New York 13035 $35—rattle; $25—pendant; $25—teething ring

24. Babies love to watch mobiles. If your infant is fussing while you need a few minutes to put a roast in the oven, a wind-up mobile might have a calming effect on him. Here's a pretty one showing five little people in flying machines. The figures have been crafted from fine natural wood and have hand-painted pilots. When the mobile is wound up, they float through the air on sturdy crossbars, which are suspended from a musical cloud. At the same time, baby hears a soft lullaby that can lull him to sleep. The mobile attaches easily to a crib or playpen.

Nursery Originals, Inc.: 280 Rand Street, Central Falls, Rhode Island 02863 $18

24

25. Create an impression on your child by stamping her name a dozen times on a piece of paper and framing it. Any local office supply dealer will make up a rubber stamp with whatever letters or words you choose. It's another way to teach your children how to spell their names—and who doesn't love to see her name in print?

$5 or over, depending on the size

25

26. One way to encourage the artists in your family is to display their work. An art-display rail made of ¾-inch veneer-core plywood has two ¼-inch-wide grooves to hold pictures or posters in place. Toys or little clay sculptures can also be perched along the rail, which measures 4 inches deep by 7 feet 6 inches long. It is finished with a clear nontoxic lacquer and can be installed easily on any wall.

PlayLearn Products Division, PCA Industries, Inc.: 2298 Grisson Drive, St. Louis, Missouri 63141 $19

26

27. Lengths of corkboard have been running around classrooms for years, displaying kids' creative talents. These map rails are 2 inches wide and come in 8-foot 6-inch, 10-foot 6-inch, and 17-foot 6-inch lengths. The self-sealing cork is encased in an aluminum channel and looks great hanging in one strip all along a bedroom wall. Arm your kids with hundreds of colorful plastic push pins, and they'll love showing off their latest "A" compositions.

The cork map rail also accommodates easy-to-attach map hooks, roller brackets, and a flag holder.

Claridge Products and Equipment, Inc.: P.O. Box 910, Harrison, Arkansas 62601 $1.25—map rail (per foot); $.40—map hook; $2.35—pair of roller brackets; $1.25—flag holder

27

28. **Many restaurateurs like this fixture because it's simple, clean-looking, and sheds plenty of light. It will be as bright hanging over a desk as in the center of a playroom. Enamel on steel, it comes in a nice assortment of colors including yellow, red, black, and white, in a variety of diameters from 12 to 20 inches. The inside is white porcelain enamel, so the light reflects well.**

Abolite Lighting, Inc.: Center Street, West Lafayette, Ohio 43845 $30—12 inches, $35—14 inches, $37—16 inches, $42—18 inches, $55—20 inches (white); $70—14 inches, $74—16 inches, $84—18 inches (red, yellow, black)

29. **This dome-shaped fixture looks almost like Abolite's, but is slightly less expensive and comes only in white. The fixture shown here has an exposed metal pendant head at top, but it also comes hidden so the dome is all white. Models are available with 12- to 18-inch diameters. Although these industrial fixtures were created to light up factories, numerous architects and designers favor them for interior use.**

Appleton Electric Co.: 1701 Wellington Avenue, Chicago, Illinois 60657 $25—12 inches; $37—18 inches

30. **Fluorescent tubes get dressed up with modern aluminum fittings in ten beautiful colors. Available in three lengths (39½, 63, or 118½ inches), SuperTube can be used as pendant lighting over a play table or fixed to the wall with brackets. When lots of lengths are joined together, you can create whole networks of illumination. Each fitting can be turned 355 degrees and the light can be directed anywhere. In addition to the pastel and primary colors, the fittings also come in aluminum.**

Scandinavian Design: 117 East 57 Street, New York, New York 10022 $126—small, $155—medium, $239—large (painted); $158—small, $188—medium, $289—large (aluminum)

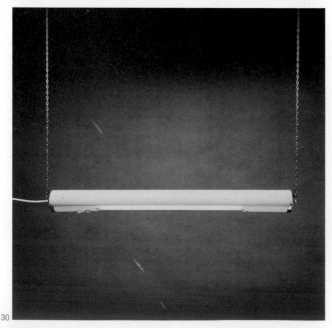

31. **Vapor-tight industrial fixtures that won't break, even when hit with a football, are surrounded with cast aluminum guards. The bulb is housed in heat-resistant glass. Each unit can take up to a 100-watt bulb and will shed**

plenty of light over a desk or play area, depending on where it's positioned. Two models are available: a bracket fixture for the wall and a ceiling version with cylindrical mount.

Stonco, Lighting Division of Keene Corp.: 2345 Vauxhall Road, Union, New Jersey 07083 $30—bracket; $24—ceiling

32. Track lighting can be put up almost anywhere—over a bed or desk, in hobby areas, on the playroom ceiling. Lightolier, a pioneer in this concept, offers a multitude of fixture shapes, materials, and accessories that can be fixed to an electrified track. The track is called Lytespan, and the individual fixtures are Lytespots.

The shape and size of a Lytespot determines the type of light projected. You may want medium or wide light to bathe large areas, or sharp-edged patterns of light to dramatize paintings or for accent lighting.

The Universal, a Lytespot preferred by architects because of its simplicity, can accept a wide variety of lamps from 30 to 300 watts. It comes in satin aluminum with matte black or white details and with either a single-arm or double-arm yoke. Both types permit horizontal adjustments up to 350 degrees and vertical up to 180 degrees.

If you want to install a single Universal Lytespot without using a track, a Monopoint fixture is available that permits surface mounting over any standard outlet box. Monopoints are ideal for accent lighting—over a reading area, for instance. They come in matte white or polished chrome.

Lytespan tracks come in satin aluminum, matte white, or matte black. The aluminum and white tracks start at 2-foot lengths, the black with 4-foot units.

Lightolier, Inc.: 346 Claremont Avenue, Jersey City, New Jersey 07305 $25—Universal Lytespot (single-arm yoke): $40—Universal Lytespot (double-arm yoke): $15—Monopoint (white); $17—Monopoint (chrome); $21—2-foot track; $32—4-foot track; $53—8-foot track

31

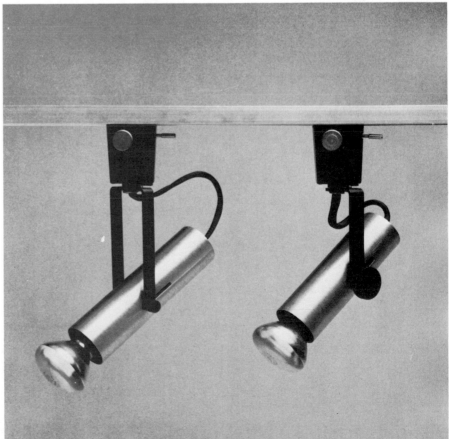

32

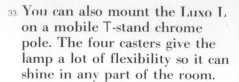

33. You can also mount the Luxo L on a mobile T-stand chrome pole. The four casters give the lamp a lot of flexibility so it can shine in any part of the room.

Luxo Lamp Corp.: Monument Park, Port Chester, New York 10573 $45—Bullet; $23—Headlight; $36—Luxo Lil (painted); $80—Luxo Lil (chrome); $46—Luxo L; $75—T-Stand

34. Gladys Goose is designed to comfort anyone who is afraid of the dark—young or old. A sweet, subtle night-light, her body is 26 inches tall and made of lightweight blow-molded plastic. The metal base holds the socket. Gladys is painted with a nontoxic paint, so it won't hurt when your little one wants to kiss her.

Heller Designs, Inc.: 460 Ogden Avenue, Mamaroneck, New York 10543 $30

35. The Japanese like their man-
made lighting to look natural.
Well-known sculptor Isamu
Noguchi creates this effect
through gracefully shaped
Japanese mino paper and
bamboo lanterns that provide
soft diffused light. Two pieces
in his Akari light sculpture
series: a popular 22-inch globe
that can float from the ceiling
and a 9- by 14-inch cube to set
on the floor or desk. There are
also globes ranging from 12
inches to 50 inches in diameter.

Akari Associates: 32–37 Vernon Boulevard, Long Island
City, New York 11106 $35—globe; $29—cube

35a

35b

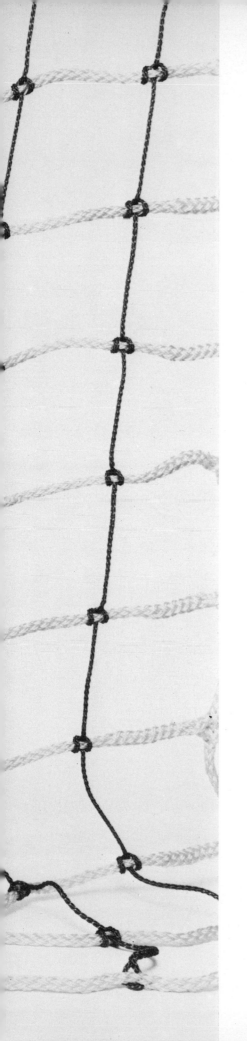

Equipment
for Indoors & Outdoors

Kids are movers: runners, throwers, jumpers, climbers, pedalers, pushers, pullers, hitters, punchers, kickers, creepers, rollers, balancers, and tumblers. And they need the physical equipment to help them develop and exercise their large muscles—inside and outside, winter and summer. Children don't want to stop moving just because it's raining out and they're confined indoors. Passive games, like building and playing house, are important to help develop fine motor skills, teach social value, and add to a child's knowledge of the world around him. But they don't satisfy a child's need to move. Expressive, physical games encourage imaginations to soar.

Physical play can and should be more than fun. It should stimulate and inspire creativity and development . . . be a way to cultivate dexterity, coordination, judgment, and intelligence.

You don't have to set up a miniature playground to make a youngster happy; some basic

2

equipment will do the trick. The amount of space you have is certainly a consideration, though not a big one. There's lots of compact equipment available that can be used indoors or out. The old saw that kids have to stay indoors and play quiet games when the weather gets bad no longer holds. Exercise should be a year-round thing. "It's important to provide a physical environment inside. Children love to finish eating, for example, and take some time out for climbing," says Marion Pasnik of New York City's Board of Education. "Children from two to three are like Tarzan and will climb anywhere—even on furniture."

Climbing apparatus can take on a variety of shapes. There are cargo nets that come in many sizes and hang from the ceiling, doorway gyms

1. Imagine what a ball your children would have if you hung a cargo climbing net in the playroom (see page 178). They could spend hours climbing, using their muscles and making believe they were mountaineers. Many physical fitness programs use climbing nets to encourage children's development. They offer a variety of movements on one piece of apparatus at varying degrees of difficulty, depending on whether the net is attached at the bottom or not. Very sturdy, this handmade net is constructed of ¾- and ⅜-inch diameter polypropylene rope with 12-inch squares. Inter-locking mesh design prevents slipping. Each vertical rope has a heavy-duty lanyard to make hanging easy. The one here is 12 feet by 12 feet, although you can have them made to order in any size. Comes in blue and yellow. It's important that a gym mat always be placed under the net.

Jayfro: P.O. Box 400, Waterford, Connecticut 06385 $213

2. Toddler gyms are popular indoor playmates on which young children enjoy testing their newly acquired coordination and large-muscle skills. This three-step climber slide also has a tunnel for crawling and hiding. Made of natural-finished hardwood with blue Masonite tunnel and slide, it measures 24½ inches wide by 62¼ inches long and 36 inches high, sized so that youngsters can easily grasp the sides and climb. The tunnel diameter is 15 inches. Several educators feel that if you were to buy one major piece of equipment for your youngster, it should be a toddler gym.

Whitney Bros. Co.: Marlborough, New Hampshire 03455 $50

with swings and ladders, compact tunnel slides. None of these takes up much space. Then there are more sophisticated climbing houses with wooden ladders, scaling ladders, rope ladders, sliding fireman's poles. These, of course, best fit into homes with a great deal of room. One parent, however, put a great big climbing house on an Oriental rug in the foyer of his apartment. It's a beautiful sculpture as well as a play device. "Tunnel slides are especially nice for children who live in apartments and rarely get to use steps," says Ethel Axelsen of the Rusk Institute.

Gym mats are another practical investment that few parents consider. They're relatively inexpensive and ideal places for tumblers, fallers, jumpers, and rollers. Give kids a reason to fling themselves to the ground and they'll go. Gym mats are a good reason. They're also fine surfaces for quiet play and can easily be put out of the way by hanging them on a wall. A punching bag and a big beach ball will satisfy the throwers, balancers, and punchers. They're perfect ways for kids to vent frustration constructively.

A bicycle machine may not take your youngster very far, but it will be a pretty close second to a real bicycle. And when you want to buy the true-to-life thing, think small. Make sure that your youngster can put his little rear on the seat and that the balls of his feet can reach the floor. A big bike for a small child will only frustrate him.

No matter what you choose, remember that well-designed equipment should stimulate children to make up their own games. Fluid units

such as climbing, balancing, and chinning structures or tubmobiles encourage movement in wild and wonderful ways. Abstracted playforms capture interest for hours. Unlike a rocking horse, which is always a rocking horse, a tubmobile can be anything a child wants—a car, train, or boat. A playground seesaw, which allows only one activity, is limiting; a rocking boat that turns upside down and becomes steps is not.

Indoor or outdoor equipment should not be so large that it's beyond the child's physical capabilities. It shouldn't overwhelm him or make demands on him that are beyond his ability level. A balance beam wouldn't be much good for a two-year-old, and he'd probably become frustrated with it.

Safety, portability, and ease of assembly are other important considerations. Generally, look for climbing units that are stationary. The child, not the equipment, should do the moving. Handholds and footholds should be safe and secure. Watch out for products that might give off splinters and inexpensive painted metal units that peel and rust.

Equipment that invites group play teaches kids to socialize. Items that offer more than one playing opportunity permit children to change games when they get bored. A big climber with bars, for instance, allows climbing, descending, chinning, and turning.

Older children, who get more involved with

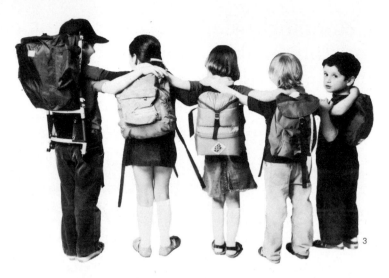

what educators call passive play, will absolutely adore inflatable boats and tents. After all, boats don't have to be confined to water and tents are still tents—even indoors.

You might be asking yourself: "Why a tent?" Think what it offers a child: a covered, enclosed, secure space for the times he wants to get away from it all. How many youngsters have you seen take a sheet, cover a table with it, and hide underneath . . . or cut "windows" into a big carton and jump inside. A tent is a small protective space inside the bigger, sometimes confusing, world. It makes a cozy place for eating, reading, playing house, or just talking. Put a little table and chair inside and your child can create his own home— at home. Tents will undoubtedly excite any child's imagination. One compact model in this chapter goes up in about ten seconds and would also be great when you want to put baby to sleep at the beach. Others are substantial enough to take on family camping trips.

3. Now no one will feel left out when the family organizes the hiking gear. These packs look like the ones grown-ups carry, but are small enough for little backs. Not just for hiking trips, the bags can also go to school.

From left to right:

The nylon Kid's Frame Pack has an S-contoured aluminum frame with a sliding adjustment that lets the pack grow with the owner. It's small enough to fit properly, but big enough to carry a complete outfit. Weighs 39 ounces.

The Bike Pack will hold two large notebooks and supplies and still have room for more in the back pocket. The zipper and all stress seams are double- or triple-stitched so impatient kids will have a hard time ripping them. This is made of 8-ounce waterproof nylon and has a double pull zipper on the main compartment. Shoulder straps are adjustable webbing and the waistband keeps the pack steady while the child bicycles. All Wilderness Experience packs come in blue, rust, or green.

The Mee Too is made of washable weatherproof nylon. It has buckles, zippers, and string so kids can learn how to tie, snap, open, and close. Shoulder straps are nylon web with buckles. There's a large outside pocket with covered zippered closure and a storm flap, too. Comes in an assortment of favorite kid colors and measures 12 by 9 by 3½ inches.

The Honey Bee has a zippered back pocket that's perfect for holding school supplies. The top opening compartment is covered with a waterproof flap so books won't get wet. Weighs 60 ounces.

The littlest one of all, called the Cricket, is designed for grade schoolers. It has a zippered front opening for toys, lunches, or supplies. Made of waterproof 8-ounce nylon in assorted colors, with double stitching where the shoulder straps and zipper are attached to the bag.

Wilderness Experience: 20120 Plummer Street, Chatsworth, California 91311 $35—Frame Pack; $13—Bike Pack; $8—Honey Bee; $7—Cricket
Camp Trails Co.: 4111 West Clarendon Avenue, Phoenix, Arizona 85019 $8—Mee Too

Inflatable boats will develop a child's creativity as well. Kids can make believe they're at sea, use the boat in the backyard as a mini pool or play space, or put a sleeping bag in it and take a nap.

No discussion of indoor/outdoor merchandise can ignore the key items you'll need to make life with a child easier: carriages, strollers, and car seats. Not all parents think they need a big carriage. They complain it's often more trouble than it's worth, and they say they'd rather have a stroller. But strollers are for strolling and don't provide the real comfort sleeping babies need. People who don't use a carriage are really looking out for their own comfort, not the infant's.

A carriage makes newborn children feel secure because it's enclosed and provides a gentle rocking motion. It can even be a baby's first bed. It's important that you have one, at least until your child is nine months old. If you can borrow a carriage, do. If you must purchase one, make sure it's the right height and weight. Petite mothers find it difficult to wield some of the heavier models. Make sure that the brakes hold securely and are simple to operate, that there are no protruding metal parts or ornaments inside or out, that the suspension system is good, and that you can see over the hood. The carriage should also be easy to collapse and open and have a safety-catch system to prevent accidental collapsing. Convertible carriages have removable bodies that can work as car beds. When used in this manner, they should be well protected and incapable of sliding around.

4. When you want to take baby along but can't be bothered with a stroller or carriage, hitch up a baby carrier. Designed to hold newborns and toddlers, this one can be worn front or back. Mothers like the front position for babies six weeks or younger—and babies like it, too, since they're closer to mother. Made of acrylic knit, this soft carrier has a padded head support and is fully adjustable and washable. The Happy Baby Carrier comes in red or blue.

Gerico, Inc.: P.O. Box 998, Boulder, Colorado 80306 $18

5. Happy travelers can ride comfortably in a frame backpack. Shoulder straps are foam-padded so mom or dad will be happy, too. The cantilevered aluminum frame transfers weight from parent's shoulders to hips. Expandable inner safety straps secure the child. The wide-angle stand opens to support the pack in a freestanding position. It's recommended for children old enough to sit up. Comes in bright green, blue, or orange cotton duck and is 2 feet high.

Gerico, Inc.: P.O. Box 998, Boulder, Colorado 80306 $23

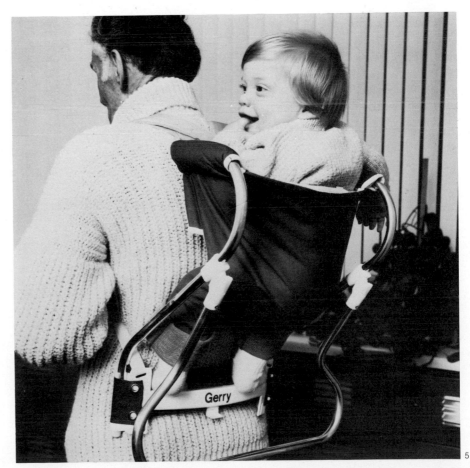

6. **Backpacks make babies feel secure and warm, and free parents to wash dishes, go shopping, or do whatever their daily routines demand. This handmade carrier, aptly called the Snugli, is a soft fabric garment worn as a front pouch, backpack, or nursing sling. It can also be expanded to carry your child until he or she is two or three years old.**

The Snugli has adjustable straps and a system of releasable tucks and darts that allow it to grow with the child. Other features include well-cushioned shoulder straps, secure buckles, detachable bubble bib, collar support for baby's head, adjustable inner pouch with full-length zipper, arm and leg holes, and full outer pouch for excellent back support. The Snugli comes in washable polyester and cotton corduroy or seersucker.

Snugli Cottage Industries, Inc.: 1150 Colorado Highway, 74 Evergreen, Colorado 80439 **$45**

Once your child is big enough to leave the carriage, it's time to get a stroller. Even then, make certain he will be comfortable. Some poorly designed models don't have proper back support. Look for a big sturdy stroller that has a four-wheel suspension system, two-wheel inside brakes, quick-release wheels, a back flap to protect the child from wind or rain, a see-through hood, padded sides, adjustable footrest and backrest, and a safety belt.

Small umbrella strollers are very popular today because they're so convenient, especially when traveling. They're also handy for older children who get tired of walking. Countless models of carriages and strollers are available. The ones in this chapter have been chosen based on function, durability, and design. Some new models have supported backs and seats and adjustable footrests. These are the best. We also recommend stainless-steel models, which, while heavier than aluminum, are more durable in the long run.

Another way to transport baby is with a car seat. There are all kinds of restraint systems for infants, toddlers, and children. Little babies need a tub-shaped seat that can cradle them in a semireclined position. It should be made of an energy-absorbing material and have a thickly padded lining to protect the head. Straps should attach over the shoulders and around the body to keep the baby secure. An infant device should be carefully fastened with the car's lap belt so that it faces the back of the car.

Some systems convert to accommodate both infants and older children up to forty pounds. A number of companies make a molded plastic shell with adapters that enable it to be used from birth to five years. These seats have safety shields that are well suited for toddlers because they provide a broad surface to catch a child in a crash.

Before purchasing any system, determine that it is the right size and gives adequate head and back support; that it is easy to put the child in and take him out of, that the straps are adjustable, sturdy, and at least 1½ inches wide; and that the metal latches do not come into contact with the child's body and are impossible for him to release. The seat should be easy to remove from the car and be suitable for use in the back seat of small cars. All seats should pass actual crash tests simulating automobile accidents from the front, side, and rear at speeds of between thirty and fifty miles per hour without putting undue strain on any part of a dummy's head, neck, or body.

Consumer Reports periodically rates all the car seats on the market, and its recommendations sometimes change from year to year. For this reason we are not showing any particular model, suggesting instead that you read safety reports before deciding what to buy. This will be one of the most important purchases you make because it involves the well-being and safety of your child.

7. Frustrated little people—or even big ones, for that matter—can vent their anxieties on a karate training bag. It's so much better than getting mad at someone else. Made of a strong synthetic and stuffed with a blended filler, the bag includes a chain and swivel for hanging. It's specially designed to take bruising chops and smashing kicks. Weighing in at 40 pounds, it's 30 by 14 inches. The bag comes in an assortment of colors from red to gray; when ordered direct, however, there is no color choice.

Everlast Sporting Goods Manufacturing Co., Inc.: 750 East 132 Street, Bronx, New York 10454 $70

8. This Satellite climber allows tots to be active at safe heights. Looking somewhat like a modern sculpture, it consists of three curved tubular steel ladders with base supports that connect to a 30-inch-diameter steel ring. The unit is 50 inches from the ground, high enough for excitement. Comes in three parts for indoor or outdoor use. Available as a portable unit or permanent installation in the backyard. The bright orange enamel is durable enough to live through rain, sleet, or snow.

Playworld Systems: P.O. Box 227, New Berlin, Pennsylvania 17855 $103

9.

9. Moms and dads have to be as comfortable wheeling around a carriage as baby is sleeping inside it. Make sure to choose a pram that offers mobility—one that can be wheeled into stores, supermarkets, even elevators. A folding chassis makes it possible to put the pram in a car or taxi should you get caught in the rain—a big advantage.

The right carriage can function inside as well as outside. Use it as baby's first bed: it can serve as well as a cradle or bassinet, and give you and baby mobility around the house. Consider putting an infant seat in the carriage and letting baby be with you whether you're eating in the dining room, den, or kitchen.

The English-made Marmet Majestic has been transporting babies for almost a quarter of a century and is the most popular model in the line because of its maneuverability in our motor-age society. It has a ribbed nylon detachable, collapsible body, sit-up backrest, and washable vinyl interior. The folding chassis is chromium-plated and fitted with 12-inch quick-release wheels and safety two-wheel brake. It comes in deep navy with a white interior, and the well-known Marmet scroll frames the hood. We chose the Majestic because of its deep body and long carrying handles. A woman alone can easily fold the chassis and carry the lightweight, soft-bodied top with baby in it.

Barclay Co.: P.O. Box 37, Teaneck, New Jersey 07666 $150

10. Umbrella strollers make a lot of sense for quick trips to the supermarket, short walks around the block, or for climbing up and down stairs. Ideal only as a second stroller, they're easy to open and close and lightweight enough so you can lift them and baby at the same time. This 6-pound Israeli-designed model is made of seamless aluminum tubes

10.

fastened by strong bolts and reportedly holds up better than most around. It has an orthopedic back support, shock absorbers for each wheel, and a safety foot brake that cannot be released by the child. The seat is cotton cloth, which absorbs perspiration and prevents skin irritation. Orange, blue, or green print or solid denim with red piping. There's an optional food utility bag for toting lunch to the park.

Octagon International, Inc.: 24 Janice Terrace, Clifton, New Jersey 07013 **$30**

11. Sturdier and wider than a conventional umbrella stroller, this Perego Super Bye Bye is still lightweight enough to maneuver easily. It has a supported seat and back, an adjustable footrest that moves as the back is reclined so baby can nap comfortably, a safety belt, and an optional hood. The back of the hood is fixed with snaps so it can be opened to let in air. Made of chrome-plated steel, it has a two-wheel brake. Exterior is blue, brown, or red nylon with washable vinyl gingham interior. Folds compactly; weighs 11½ pounds.

Barclay Co.: P. O. Box 37, Teaneck, New Jersey 07666 **$55**

12. Large strollers are great for children who have learned to sit. One of the best on the market, this Perego Elba model has a two-wheel brake system and shackle gear. A reclining adjustable back with adjustable footrest lets your toddler relax comfortably. Comes with a summer canopy which has a see-through winter attachment to protect against rain and wind. White balloon tires and chrome-plated steel construction. Interior is washable vinyl in navy, brown, mulberry, or gingham with complementary exteriors. Folds easily for car travel or storage.

Barclay Co.: P.O. Box 37, Teaneck, New Jersey 07666 **$80**

11

12

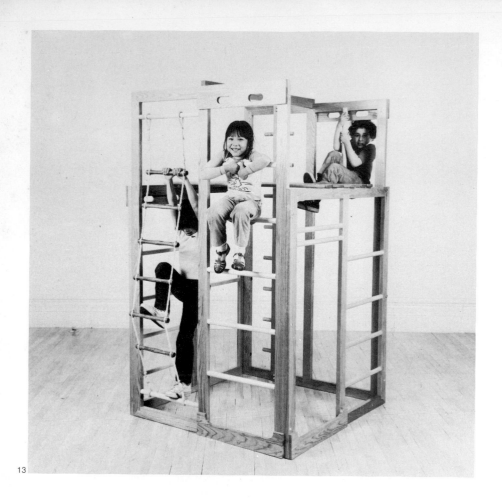

13.

13. Young climbers will never tire of this climbing house, with its wooden ladders, scaling ladder, rope ladder, fireman's pole, chinning and horizontal bars, and tumbling bar. When they're done satisfying their climbing instincts for the day, they can make believe it's a real house. Three cleated boards fit across the top as a roof or can be laid across the rungs to make a solid play floor. Constructed of 1⅛-inch by 2¾-inch straight-grained northern maple with 1⅛-inch hardwood rungs, it has mortised joints, braces on every panel, and countersunk holes to shield plated hardware. Comes with socket wrench for easy assembly. Measures 7 feet high and 4 feet 4 inches long. Put a mattress within the structure or next to it to create a fabulous sleeping environment for your youngster.

Childcraft Education Corp.: 20 Kilmer Road, Edison, New Jersey 08817 $550

14. Although this solid maple junior gym is ideal for the great outdoors, it's compact enough to go inside where city kids can enjoy it, too. A platform near the top allows safe entry onto the detachable 6-foot slide. A hinged door makes kids feel like they're hiding. The gym measures 38 by 38 by 48 inches high. Folds flat for easy storage.

Playworld Systems: P.O. Box 227, New Berlin, Pennsylvania 17855 $138

14.

15. Another, slightly different toddler gym, this one has an open crawling tunnel and smaller dimensions. It will foster self-confidence in children who are timid about testing physical abilities. Made of hardwood and Masonite, it is 18½ inches wide by 60 inches long by 33½ inches high.

Childcraft Education Corp.: 20 Kilmer Road, Edison, New Jersey 08817 $50

16. Two- to four-year-olds can rock back and forth making believe they're sailors in this well-constructed rocking boat. Or they can turn it over and pretend they're mountaineers on the set of climbing steps. The unit is particularly useful in apartments where there are no steps for tots to practice on. Made of hardwood, it comes completely assembled and measures 47¾ inches long by 23 inches wide by 12 inches high. It's finished for outdoor use.

Childcraft Education Corp.: 20 Kilmer Road, Edison, New Jersey 08817 $73

17. Trampolines encourage children to be wild and funny, and help develop coordination. This 4- by 6-foot model will take on two bouncing youngsters at once. Its frame is 1-inch galvanized pipe. The open ends are fitted with plastic glides and rubber crutch tips. There's a double-covered shock cord and vinyl-coated red nylon surface.

Even when adults are using big trampolines, it's always necessary to have "spotters." So when your kids are using this one, make sure at least two other children are standing at the sides—in case the jumper should get carried away. If used properly, the trampoline is as safe as other gym equipment.

Playworld Systems: P.O. Box 227, New Berlin, Pennsylvania 17855 $180

15

16

17

18. This wood swing set is costly but will undoubtedly outlast less expensive metal versions—without becoming a rusty eyesore. And chances are no one will ever get bored on this Jungle-End Swing Set because it offers so many activities for toddlers to 12-year-olds.

The set is made of three ladders: two 8-foot side ladders supporting a 10-foot overhead ladder. A child can climb the side ladders or swing hand over hand along the overhead ladder.

Three fixtures hang from the overhead ladder: a trapeze bar with large aluminum rings; a glider that seats two children back to back; and a rubberized fabric sling seat. All three pieces can be changed or adjusted up and down by moving the ropes to which each is attached. At one end there's the climbing jungle and ladders, with plenty of room inside the jungle for access to the optional slide... and for gymnastics. An 8-foot rope climbing net and a sliding fireman's pole mount on the sides. Two cleated platforms fit anywhere inside the jungle that children wish to put them.

All uprights and ladder rails on the set are durable wood painted forest green, and rungs are natural maple with a nonslip finish. The overall unit is 8 feet high and 13 feet long, not including the optional 8-foot slide. Other swings are also available, including ones for baby and toddler.

The set is relatively simple for two people to install using nothing more than a wrench and hammer. There's no need to dig holes or use cement, so relocation is easy. Oak stakes 16 inches long anchor the four corners on top of the ground, and 8-foot-wide base supports give the necessary stability for safe swinging.

Child Life Play Specialties, Inc.: 55 Whitney Street, Holliston, Massachusetts 01746 $250; $310—with slide

19. Cleverly designed to excite children's imaginations, these three colorful curved sections can combine to form a circle, a reclining seat, or whatever a child wills. Red, yellow, and blue unbreakable polyethylene.

Childcraft Education Corp.: 20 Kilmer Road, Edison, New Jersey 08817 $60

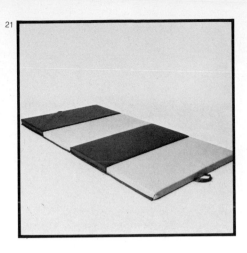

20. Kids always love to show off their gym skills by doing somersaults or handstands on the living room floor. Put a gym mat down and they'll be able to tumble all day. Nissen's mats are recognized by the professionals. The core is a combination of Ethafoam and polyurethane, giving it the necessary softness for younger children. The washable nylon-reinforced vinyl covering comes in blue and tan, and is treated with a special compound which helps prevent the spread of infection-causing bacteria. The mat is lightweight enough for a child to fold and store easily. It's 4 feet by 6 feet.

Put the mat out of the way by attaching it to a Velcro wall strip which accommodates Velcro fasteners on the mat's ends. A steel-reinforced vinyl sheath with nylon hooks holds the Velcro.

Nissen, subsidiary of Walter Kidde and Co., Inc.: 930 27 Avenue S.W., Cedar Rapids, Iowa 52406 **$90**

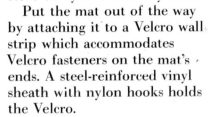
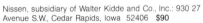

21. The Jaylite mat, measuring 3 feet by 6 feet by 2 inches thick, has been designed for little gymnasts. It's made of six-pound density bonded foam with a vinyl-coated nylon cover in six basic colors, with a striped top and solid color bottom. The mat comes with two vinyl-coated handles and folds into a neat package 2 feet by 3 feet by 6 inches thick for carrying. Custom sizes are available at $2.60 per square foot.

Jayfro Corp.: P.O. Box 400, Waterford, Connecticut 06385 **$49**

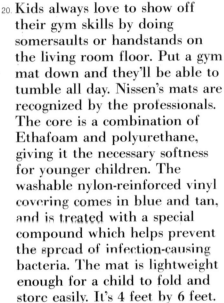

22

23

24

22. A less expensive lightweight mat made of washable heavy-duty vinyl-supported fabric with nylon sidewalls and handles. The filler is polyfoam, either 1 or 2 inches thick. The one shown here measures 4 feet by 6 feet 2 inches, but sizes are available up to 5 feet by 10 feet. Red, green, or blue bottom with gray top—there is no color choice.

Everlast Sporting Goods Manufacturing Co., Inc.: 750 East 132 Street, Bronx, New York 10454 $56

23. Hang a gym mat on a free wall at home and throw it down when you or your family want to exercise or accommodate a sleepover guest. The core of this mat is 2-inch-thick high-density Durofoam, covered with 100 percent washable vinyl-coated nylon. It will stand up to strenuous use. Comes in gray only. The 4- by 6-foot size is shown here, but you can get it as large as 6 feet by 12 feet.

Everlast Sporting Goods Manufacturing Co., Inc.: 750 East 132 Street, Bronx, New York 10454 $88

24. Rubbermaid makes a heavy-duty mat that can protect floors when the children are going wild. Its ribbed-cushioned vinyl makes seating easier. It would also be a good place to park the baby carriage when you come in from an unexpected shower. Available in a number of sizes. The one here is ⅜-inch by 3 feet by 5 feet. Gray.

Rubbermaid Commercial Products, Inc.: Winchester, Virginia 22601 $26

25. Sometimes big city children don't get to exercise as much as their suburban friends. Since bicycle riding is one of children's favorite sports, why not arrange for them to bicycle indoors? A bicycle machine may not be exactly the same as the real McCoy, but it will be a good alternative. Here's one that features a speedometer and odometer, adjustable padded seat, ball-bearing pedals, and chain guard. It has a 20-inch

chrome wheel and tire, heavy-duty welded frame, and chrome handlebars. And no one says you can't use it once the children have gone to bed. A tension roller lets you go on smooth or vigorous rides.

Vita Master Industries, Inc.: 455 Smith Street, Brooklyn, New York 11231 $110

26. Just about anyone can ride a bicycle, even a two-year-old—as long as the size of the bike relates to the size of the rider. Your child should be able to place his backside comfortably on the bike seat and still touch the ground with the balls of his feet. That way the child will feel secure if he loses his balance when the bike tips. When first learning to ride, he'll be able to stop the bike with his feet without having to use the brakes.

Small bikes usually don't have the crossbar found on men's bicycle frames. This is just as well, since it only hampers a child's ability to mount and dismount.

Here are two small bikes for small people: the Chico Pico and the Atala. Chico Pico is lighter weight and not as sturdy as Atala, and is therefore less expensive. Chico comes with 10-, 12-, or 14-inch wheels; Atala has 10-, 14-, or 16-inch wheels. Generally, a two-year-old is most comfortable with 10-inch wheels, a three-year-old with 12-inch, and a four- or five-year-old with 14-inch wheels.

Stuyvesant Bicycle Distributors: 349 West 14 Street, New York, New York 10014 $29.95—all Chico Pico models; $69.95—10-inch Atala; $79.95—16-inch Atala

25

26 a

26 b

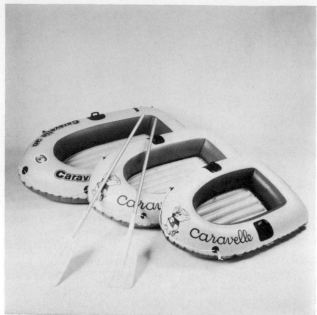

27a

27b

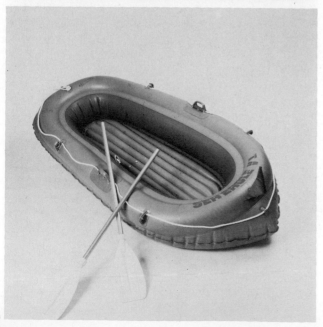

28

27. Inflatable boats can also live out of water. Use them as seats or portable beds. Take them to the beach, throw in some sand, and let the kids play. They can also become backyard splash pools for babies. These are made of Neopryl, a combination of plastic and synthetic rubber that is unaffected by sun, salt water, and chlorine. Since they've been designed as boats, they have multiple air chambers, lifelines, built-in oar locks, and inflatable floors. Nine different sizes, ranging from a child's boat to an 11-foot family boat. Shown are the three smallest.

Sevylor U.S.A., Inc.: 6802 Watcher Street, Los Angeles, California 90040 $15—Caravelle child; $20—Junior; $36—One-man; $12—small oars; $4—small pump

28. Children don't need water to make believe they're at sea; this one- or two-man 6-foot 8-inch dinghy will be more than enough to excite their imaginations. Turned upside down, it's just right for jumping on. Then when nap time comes, the kids can rest in it, too. It comes with oar clasps, all-around rope lacing, air pressure gauge, and repair kit, just in case you want to take it on family outings on the real water. Weighs 12 pounds and can hold up to 350 pounds.

Leisure Imports, Inc.: 104 Arlington Avenue, St. James, New York 11780 $69

29. Kids love to throw covers over chairs and hide underneath. That way, they can crawl into their own little world, away from all the grown-ups. Think how much they'd enjoy having a tent right in the bedroom. It probably would become their second home. And, of course, tents are also great when the kids want to sleep outdoors or go camping.

Called the ten-second tent because it takes just that long to go up, this dome-shaped free-standing shelter is made of nylon with a cotton crown. It has a built-in frame like an umbrella, three-way zippered screen door, and two rear screen windows. Folds into a small package with its own carrying case. Take it to the beach to protect a napping baby from the sun.

Sunshine Cover and Tarp., Inc.: 20310 Plummer Street, Chatsworth, California 91311 $75

29

30. Another compact model, this tent is self-supporting and is suspended from an aluminum frame with shock cords. A modified A-type door works in conjunction with the large rear window for controlled cross-circulation. Zippers are nylon coil. Ripstop nylon is used in the wrap around the floor, up the sides, and on the roof. The tent also has a map pocket and interior rings for a clothesline so the kids really can make believe it's their home. The floor measures 5 feet 3 inches by 7 feet 2 inches and the height is 42 inches. Comes in orange with blue or green with yellow. Among the relatively inexpensive freestanding tents, this shelter is one of the most popular with serious campers.

Eureka! Tent, Inc.: 625 Conklin Road, Box 966, Binghamton, New York 13902 $98

30

31

32

33

31. Children will love making
    believe that this circular
    tubmobile is a boat, train, car,
    or spaceship. Four ball-bearing
    swivel casters permit movement
    in any direction. Heavy
    vulcanized fiber sides are firmly
    riveted and reinforced with
    metal rim and handles. The
    floor is a sheet of heavy-gauge
    steel. Comes in bright orange.
    Twenty-four inches in diameter
    and 15 inches high. Comfortably
    holds two tots or lots of toys.

    Childcraft Education Corp.: 20 Kilmer Road, Edison, New
    Jersey 08817 $45

32. Some kids live in big city
    apartments and need all the
    exercise they can get. If yours is
    one of them, an indoor gym will
    help fill that need. This all-in-
    one unit hangs in any doorway
    and includes a flexible belt
    swing, steel trapeze rings with

plastic grips, blocked climbing rope, and hitching rings. Children can adjust the height by themselves.

Child Life Play Specialties, Inc.: 55 Whitney Street, Holliston, Massachusetts 01746 **$25**

33. This 11-inch-high activity dolly encourages youngsters to use their leg muscles. The seat, made of natural-finish birch plywood, is fastened to a heavy-gauge steel tubing frame. The hard rubber swivel casters won't mar the floor if anyone wants to play train.

Playworld Systems: P.O. Box 227, New Berlin, Pennsylvania 17855 **$15**

34

34. If you can't bring your child outdoors, bring the outdoors in with a mobile sandbox. Mounted on two glided rear legs and two front ball-bearing casters, it can easily be transported from the backyard to the garage at the end of the day so the sand won't get "dirty." It's made of metal, painted in bright yellow, and measures 32 inches long by 24 inches wide by 8 inches deep.

Playworld Systems: P.O. Box 227, New Berlin, Pennsylvania 17855 **$45**

35. Little bodies can roll around and have a ball on this wonderful gym scooter. Constructed from foam polypropylene, it has side handles and hand guards so a youngster can get a good safe grip. Four 2-inch-diameter ball-bearing swivel casters move easily on carpet and won't mar resilient flooring. Measures 12 by 12 by 1½ inches.

Jayfro: P.O. Box 400, Waterbury, Connecticut 06385 **$16**

35

36. Kids can create fantasy worlds with the simplest objects. A ¾-inch plywood board on four swiveling wheels can be a car, train, boat, raft—anything a child's imagination decides. They'll also use the dolly to transport toys and friends from room to room. Measures 23½ inches long by 19½ inches wide.

American Montessori Society: 150 Fifth Avenue, New York, New York 10011 **$65**

36

37. Your child can develop muscular strength and balance and have just plain fun with this sturdy inflatable beach ball. Wonderful for group play when pushing, rolling, and stretching are encouraged. Its large 36-inch size and looped cord makes it ideal for hanging up and hitting. Kick it around at home when feelings get aggressive.

Ccvylor U.S.A., Inc.: 6802 Watchor Street, Los Angeles, California 90040 $16

38. Balls, like bikes, should correspond to a youngster's age and size. Give a six-year-old a big professional football, and you'll get a frustrated quarterback. To teach a five- to ten-year-old child proper ball handing and passing, team him up with a scaled down, junior football and watch him master it.

If your child prefers another sport, there's also a selection of soccer, basket, and playground balls—all available in various sizes for your growing athlete.

The three soccer balls here are made of rugged synthetic leather. The biggest, Breakaway #5, is used by many soccer clubs across the country and is designed for thirteen-year-olds to adults. Nine-to-twelve year-olds will do well with Future Star #4, and five-to-eight-year-olds will prefer Jr. Playmaker #3.

The bigger football is official size and weight, ideal for junior high kids and up; the Jr. football, 10½ inches long, is for young players up to ten years old.

The larger basketball is also official size and weight for the bigger guys; the Jr. basketball has a 28-inch circumference and weighs 19 ounces.

Playground balls are ideal indoors and out. They are softer and safer than regular balls. Still, they have lots of bounce and are weighty enough to really move when kicked. They come in diameters ranging from 5 inches to 16 inches.

AMF Voit, subsidiary of AMF Inc.: 3801 South Harbor Boulevard, Santa Ana, California 92704   Soccer balls: all are around $31; Footballs: around $19; Basketballs: $21.50, $14.50; Playground balls: $3.50 to $11

About the Authors

Geri Brin and Linda Foa met while both were editors at *Home Furnishings Daily*, the trade newspaper of the industry. Linda wrote a column called "F.Y.I.," and Geri edited the housewares section. Since then, they have both written articles for newspapers and magazines on furnishing trends, from the classics to the new "high tech" look for the home.

Linda works out of her home, where she does freelance writing. She is married and has two children. Geri is publicity manager for Norelco Consumer Products Division. She too is married, and the Brins are expecting their first child in early 1979. Both authors live in New York.